Stark Young

Twayne's United States Authors Series

Kenneth Eble, Editor

University of Utah

TUSAS 463

STARK YOUNG
(1881–1963)

Stark Young

By John Pilkington

University of Mississippi

Twayne Publishers • *Boston*

CARNEGIE LIBRARY
LIVINGSTONE COLLEGE
SALISBURY, N. C. 28144

Stark Young

John Pilkington

Copyright © 1985 by G. K. Hall & Company
All Rights Reserved
Published by Twayne Publishers
A Division of G. K. Hall & Company
70 Lincoln Street
Boston, Massachusetts 02111

Book Production by Elizabeth Todesco
Book Design by Barbara Anderson

Printed on permanent/durable acid-free
paper and bound in the United States of
America.

Library of Congress Cataloging in Publication Data

Pilkington, John, 1918–
    Stark Young.

    (Twayne's United States authors series; TUSAS 463)
    Bibliography: p. 152
    Includes index.
    1. Young, Stark, 1881–1963—Criticism and interpretation.
I. Title. II. Series.
PS3547.O6Z82 1985   818'.5209   84–27957
ISBN 0–8057–7403–3

818.52
Y76

To L. K. P. and C. K. P.

117903

Contents

About the Author

Born in Jacksonville, Florida, John Pilkington was educated at Centre College (A.B., 1940), Johns Hopkins University (1940–41), and Harvard University (M.A., 1947; Ph.D., 1952). In 1952 he joined the faculty of the University of Mississippi as assistant professor of English, becoming associate professor in 1956 and professor in 1960. From 1970 to 1977 he served as associate dean of the graduate school, and in 1977 he was designated by the University of Mississippi as its first Distinguished Professor of English.

He is the author of two other volumes in the Twayne U. S. Authors Series: *Francis Marion Crawford* (1964) and *Henry Blake Fuller* (1971). In 1975 his *Stark Young: A Life in the Arts, Letters, 1900–1962* was published by the Louisiana State University Press, and in 1981 his *The Heart of Yoknapatawpha* was published by the University Press of Mississippi.

In 1974 Professor Pilkington's Stark Young volumes won the Jules F. Landry Award. In 1979 Professor Pilkington received the Distinguished Alumni Award from Centre College and in 1982 the honorary degree of Doctor of Humane Letters from the College of Idaho.

Preface

As poet, playwright, critic, novelist, translator, and painter, Stark Young has left his mark upon the arts in America. His contemporaries, both admirers and detractors, conceded that he stood for something unique and valuable in American culture. Yet, although his work has received attention in most histories of the American theatre, in analyses of the Southern Agrarians, in discussions of Civil War fiction, and in studies of the Southern literary renaissance, no single volume has been devoted to the totality of his writings and his position in the arts. In keeping with the format of the Twayne U. S. Authors Series, I have endeavored to write such a book. This work is not a biography; on the contrary, biographical material has been restricted to those aspects of his life that have a significant bearing upon his writings. Not every work written by Young, moreover, has been examined in detail. Several minor works—examples are *Encaustics, The Three Fountains,* and *Sweet Times and the Blue Policeman*—have been slighted to provide space for a fuller treatment of writings that have major importance either as revealing his central ideas or different facets of his artistic productions. Young's more than a thousand pieces of criticism, sketches, and essays in the *New Republic, Theatre Arts,* and other periodicals are represented primarily through analysis of his volumes on the theater, which were mainly assembled from such articles. Within these limitations, I have sought to provide readers with a survey of Stark Young's career, the content of his best and most characteristic writing, and an evaluation of his place in the Southern literary movement. Above all, I have tried to define Stark Young's "position" relative to the arts.

Much of the research for this book was accomplished in the preparation of the two-volume edition of his correspondence that I edited with commentary, published by the Louisiana State University Press in 1975. To this press and to the late William McKnight Bowman, I am indebted for permission to publish excerpts from Young's correspondence that throw light upon his writings. I also gratefully acknowledge permission from the following publishers to print quotations from works by Stark Young; copyright dates appear in parentheses following titles: To Charles Scribner's Sons, *The Flower in Drama* (1923, 1951); *Glamour* (1925, 1953); *Heaven Trees* (1926, 1954); *Theatre Practice* (1926, 1954); *The Torches Flare* (1928, 1956); *River House* (1929, 1962); *So Red the Rose* (1934, 1962); *The Pavilion* (1951, 1979); and to Harper and Row, *I'll Take My Stand* (1930, 1958). For permission to publish excerpts from Stark Young's *The Theater* (1927, 1957), I thank Lewis M. Isaacs, Seymour S. Sussman, and Farrar, Straus & Giroux.

I wish to thank Evans Harrington and Gerald Walton, friends, colleagues, and scholars, for reading the manuscript and making valuable suggestions about it. To my wife, who has patiently listened to my difficulties, helped me with more than one knotty problem, and typed the manuscript, I owe more than I can adequately express.

John Pilkington

University of Mississippi

Chronology

1927   *The Theater* and translation of Machiavelli's *Mandragola*.

1928   *The Torches Flare.*

1929   *River House.*

1930   Completes "Not in Memoriam, But in Defense" for *I'll Take My Stand.* Herbert Croly dies.

1933   Problems at *New Republic* increase. Controversy over handling of Scottsboro case.

1934   *So Red the Rose.*

1935   *Feliciana.*

1936   Stark Young Robertson dies.

1938   Translates Chekhov's *The Sea Gull* for the Lunts.

1939   Writes *Belle Isle (Artemise).* Travels with Lunts.

1942   Bitterness over *Belle Isle* increases. Works on paintings.

1943   Exhibition of paintings in New York.

1946   Exhibition of paintings at Rehn Galleries and museums.

1947   Resigns from *New Republic.*

1948   Resigns from *Theatre Arts. Immortal Shadows.*

1951   *The Pavilion.*

1953   New edition of *So Red the Rose* with introduction by Donald Davidson.

1955–1956   Chekhov translations produced at Fourth Street Theater. New edition combines *The Flower in Drama* and *Glamour* in a single volume.

1958   New edition of *The Theater.*

1959   Lectures at Wellesley and Harvard. Suffers stroke. Receives Distinguished Service Award from South Eastern Theatre Conference.

1962   Julia Young Robertson, sister, dies on 20 December.

1963   Stark Young dies on 6 January.

Chapter One

Southern Origins

About fifty miles south of Memphis, Tennessee, and thirty-five miles northwest of Oxford, Mississippi, lies Como, Mississippi, birthplace of Stark Young. In 1880, the year before Young was born, the population of Como numbered 149 persons, the majority of whom, families of the first white settlers or their descendants, lived along its two main streets; ten years later, when the census was again taken, its population had increased by only twenty-nine persons. In most respects, the community seems an unlikely place in which to seek the origins of a many-faceted genius who began as a poet and successively became a university professor, playwright, drama critic, Broadway direc-tor, novelist, translator, and painter, known throughout artistic circles as a brilliant conversationalist, a sophisticated New York intellectual, and a creative artist. Yet in the stable, rural, agrarian Mississippi society of cotton planters and landowning farmers, Stark Young spent his childhood and formed the attitudes and personality configurations that dominated his life and creative work for more than eighty years.

Precisely what the joys and pains of that Como childhood meant to Young, he sought to define in the opening pages of his autobiography, *The Pavilion* (1951). Young recalled a small waterfall made in front of his house each time heavy rains over-flowed a hidden culvert. Eagerly he would watch the rapidly moving water and listen to its sound until the little Como water-fall became "all water falling everywhere, all the crystalline whiteness and purity of water, and all the voice of water in the natural world."[1] That small waterfall thus became for Young both a symbol and essence throughout the remainder of his life. When he saw Niagara, the falls of the American West, and others at Tivoli and in Mexico, they became for him exten-sions of what he already knew. Although Young, characteristi-cally, did not press the metaphor, his meaning is clear: the

essence of life, especially the principles of right living, which
formed the core of the Southern humanism that he learned
from his family in Como, could be transported wherever he
went.

At the center of Young's values lies the family, for in it he
believed that the individual, as he often said, best lived "the
life of the affections." The phrase contains the key to his basic
attitudes; and although his desire for family living at times seems
to have reached a high emotional pitch, paradoxically he never
enjoyed a family life of his own except in his Como childhood.
In later life a homosexual, he never married and participated
only intermittently in his sister's household. He focused his desires for the continuance of his family upon his sister's son,
who shared with him the kinship with the McGehees on his
mother's side and the Young ancestors of his father. These two
families exerted a controlling influence upon Young's life.

The Youngs

Young's father, Alfred Alexander Young (1847–1925), was
a doctor. His family had originated in England. In the War of
the Spanish Succession, the Youngs fought under the duke of
Marlborough; and shortly after the Battle of Blenheim in 1704,
Michael Cadet Young, a younger son, emigrated to Isle of Wight
County, Virginia, was married, and became the father of a large
family. His fourth son, Thomas Young (1732–1828), turned
south to North Carolina, where he married twice and became
the progenitor of a large family. Two of his sons, William and
Henry, followed the westward trails into Tennessee, where one
of them, probably William, became the father of William Henry
Young (1813–88), whom Stark Young remembered as "Grandfather Young." Shortly after Alfred Alexander Young was born,
the family moved to Marshall County, near Holly Springs, Mississippi.

In 1863, at the age of sixteen, after a childhood spent in
the vicinity of Holly Springs, Alfred Alexander Young enlisted
in the Third Regiment Mississippi Cavalry, under the command
of Colonel John McGuirk. Although at the time this force was
not a part of the regular Confederate Army, like most of the
irregular forces, it was later mustered into the regular service.
Young participated in the fighting around Memphis and Holly

Springs and in maneuvers to support General Nathan B. Forrest's raid into Tennessee. Young also fought in battles near Vicksburg, Jackson, and Atlanta. After the surrender of the Confederate forces on 4 May 1865 at Citronelle, Alabama, he was paroled and walked back to his home in Marshall County.

In the fall of 1866, a year after the University of Mississippi reopened after the war, Alfred Alexander Young began his college education with the 243 other students registered in that session. He took the prescribed freshman studies, joined the Sigma Chi Fraternity, and participated in one of the two literary societies. Shortly before Christmas in his sophomore year, however, he left abruptly, probably because of financial difficulties. He went home to farm and to serve as apprentice to a country doctor. During the academic years 1868–69 and 1869–70, he attended the University of Pennsylvania Medical School, wrote a thesis dealing with female diseases, and received his degree in medicine. He returned to Mississippi and moved to Como to practice. Ten years later, in 1880, he married Mary Clark Starks (1858–90) in the same little Fredonia Church, about a mile from Como, where her mother and father had been married in 1848.

Stark Young was devoted to his father, proud of his record in the Confederate Army, and sympathetic to his weaknesses. As a child, Stark often accompanied his father when he visited patients who lived out in the country, and during the long buggy rides Doctor Young endeavored to inculcate in his young son Southern ways of thinking, good manners, consideration for others, and compassion for the poor, the sick, and the friendless. Doctor Young's patients at times thought him garrulous, even gossipy, especially as he grew older; and after he moved to Oxford they turned in increasing numbers to younger and perhaps more skillful practitioners. Although aware of these matters, Stark Young never ceased to praise his father's integrity, his conscientiousness in respect to the practice of his profession, and his sympathy for those in trouble.

The McGehees

Affectionate as Young was toward his father's family, his ties to the Youngs were never so strong as his feelings for the McGehees on his mother's side. Mary Clark Starks was the daughter

of Caroline Charlotte McGehee (1821–61) and Stephen Gilbert
Starks (1816–59), a Methodist circuit rider who traveled
through north Mississippi preaching at various churches, including the Fredonia Church at Como, the home of the north Mississippi branch of the McGehee family. Starks had been born in
Vermont, and Caroline Charlotte's father disliked the prospect
of his daughter marrying a Northern man. To prevent an elope-
ment, he locked her into her room, but she found a way to
Memphis. After their marriage in 1848, they moved to Holly
Springs, where the Reverend Starks became widely respected
for his preaching and contributions to female education.

The McGehees had been leaders in the affairs of Panola
County almost since it had been organized out of the land ceded
to the government in 1836 by the Chickasaw Indians under
the Treaty of Pontotoc. The ancestor of the American branch
of the family, James McGregor, a younger son of the McGregor
clan in Scotland, had emigrated into Virginia early in the seven-
teenth century and changed his name to McGehee. For several
generations, the McGehees accumulated wealth and position
in Prince Edward County, Virginia; but soon after the American
Revolution, Micajah McGehee (1745–1811) moved his wife
and children to a settlement along the Broad River in Georgia.
Micajah was a strong, blunt, brandy-loving Methodist, and his
wife was a thrifty, energetic, pioneering woman. The couple
had fourteen children, almost all of whom lived to adulthood.

As rapidly as Micajah's sons reached maturity, he gave each
one $5,000 and seven slaves and told him to make his own
living. Several took their inheritance and turned westward; others remained in Georgia. Three of the boys, Edward (1786–
1880), John (1789–1870), and Hugh (1793–1855), drove their
wagons into Mississippi. Edward and John became Stark Young's
great-uncles; Hugh was his grandfather. All three men became
successful planters, prominent figures in the state, and owners
of large acreages and many slaves. As a small boy, Stark Young
heard so many stories about them that they seemed to him
heroes from his own family separated from him only by a gap
in time. He had the sense of belonging to a large clan who
loved him. For Young the memory of his ancestors was almost
"second nature." In *The Pavilion* he wrote that his Uncle Hugh
would have thought it "strange if I had cared nothing about

his father, whom I had never seen but whom he had loved.
. . . At what point do we cease to care one way or the other
about people? he would have asked" (78). To Young this feeling
of continuity was in no sense ancestor worship.

Near Woodville, in southern Mississippi, Edward McGehee,
whose thousand slaves made him one of the largest slaveholders
in the state, established "Bowling Green" plantation. In addition
to a splendid mansion, he built the West Feliciana Railroad,
operated a cotton gin, and donated generously to educational
institutions. Married three times, he fathered eighteen children.
Throughout the region he was known as "Judge McGehee."
Much of his wealth was lost during the Civil War when Federal
soldiers burned his mansion in sight of his wife and children
and destroyed his railroad by heating the rails and twisting them
around trees. Of the once magnificent "Bowling Green," only
the three columns that supported the main doorway and the
brick walk leading to the entrance now remain; but many of
the features of the building, as well as of Edward's career, survive
in Stark Young's *So Red the Rose.*

Edward's two brothers, John and Hugh, stopped their westward progress in Panola County, near Como, in north Mississippi. John became a prosperous planter, a leader in the
community, and the founder of the Fredonia Methodist Church.
He was known for his charity and his efforts to alleviate the
sufferings of the poor. Two of his eleven children, Miles (1813–
65) and Tabitha Ann (1818–79), have prominent roles in Stark
Young's fiction. Miles appears as head of a Southern planter's
family. Tabitha Ann married Dr. Charles F. Dandridge, a name
Young used without change in his novels.

In 1839 Hugh McGehee also settled in Panola County and
began a career that bears resemblances to that of his older
brother Edward. Like his brother, Hugh soon acquired considerable land and slaves, and in the next few years he became prominent in the Como community as a successful cotton planter and
lumberman. To transport these products to marketing centers,
he joined several friends to build a railroad from Memphis to
Grenada. Ultimately, this road became a link in the Illinois-
Central system from Chicago to New Orleans. Throughout Stark
Young's boyhood and even into the 1920s and 1930s, the train
could always be flagged to stop at "McGehee's Crossing," near

the Tate County line, about a mile north of Como. Young greatly prized a Confederate bank note bearing an engraving of his grandfather standing beside the "Hugh McGehee Locomotive." Hugh fathered eleven children, three of whom—Caroline Charlotte (1821–61), Abner Francis (1828–92), and Hugh (1834–1915)—influenced Young's life and work. In *The Pavilion,* Young includes a lively account of their lives, opinions, and, at times, eccentricities.

At the beginning of the Civil War, Abner Francis McGehee (Young's great-uncle) owned at least three sections of land near Como and more than a hundred slaves. During the war, he suffered serious financial losses, but in the following decades his home remained a gathering place for the numerous members of the McGehee family. As a young boy, Stark Young often sat on the front porch of Abner's house to listen to the talk that Young later thought was the origin of his Southern humanism. Abner's daughter, Caroline Charlotte, was a particular favorite of Young; in the scores of letters he wrote to her after he left Como, he always addressed her affectionately as "Cousin Cad." She is not to be confused, however, with the Caroline Charlotte McGehee who was the sister of Abner and Hugh and the grandmother of Young.

Hugh McGehee (1834–1915), Abner's brother and Stark Young's great-uncle, whom Young called "Uncle Hugh," inherited large tracts of land in Panola and Tippah counties. As a young man, he dressed in the latest fashion, enjoyed the luxuries of life at the area resorts, and attended the University of Mississippi, where he learned to admire Plato and studied religious history. In 1865 he married Julia Valette Little (1845–1930), settled down, and spent the remainder of his life humoring his wife's extravagances. Late in life, after his fortune diminished, he gradually withdrew from local society. He was extremely fond of Stark Young and often sat with him for hours at a time, talking about Southern manners and Southern people. From him, Young obtained much of his lifelong concern for his family and the importance of the continuity of family life. From "Uncle Hugh," Young learned the answer to the question, "Who am I?"

Through his connections with this huge, sprawling family, Stark Young could have said that he was related to almost half the population of Como. During the remainder of his life, even while living in Texas and New York, he kept up with their activities. Beyond question, the influence of the McGehees upon his life and career can scarcely be overestimated. More than anything else, they made Young a Southerner for life; they gave his artistic work a Southern cast; and they instilled in him a faithful adherence to Southern values, Southern traditions, and Southern standards that permeated his outlook upon life. Throughout his work, the reflection of his boyhood association with the McGehees, their role in defining the individual, and the feeling of continuity that he felt toward these people—"my people," as he called them—can be understood as the legacy of the McGehees to their Como "cousin." With remarkable objectivity, he recognized the McGehees' virtues and their weaknesses. As his delineation of them in his novels and in *The Pavilion* demonstrates, he could be severe, even caustic, in his criticism of their faults; nevertheless, the McGehee family represents a major factor in the formation of Young's outlook and attitudes.

After moving to Holly Springs with her husband (the Reverend Stephen Gilbert Starks) Caroline Charlotte (McGehee) Starks bore him four children: Sarah Gilbert (1854–1939), Frances Scott (1857–1931), Mary Clark (1858–90)—she was to be the mother of Stark Young—and Hugh McGehee, who died early in life. In 1859 the Reverend Starks died, and two years later, Caroline died. The four children, now orphans, were sent back to Como to live with their uncle, Hugh McGehee. On 28 December 1880 Mary (Mollie) Clark Starks married Alfred Alexander Young, and on 11 October 1881 Stark Young was born in Como, Mississippi. On 10 June 1884 Mollie Young gave birth to a daughter, Julia McGehee Young; in 1886 she had a son who died as an infant.

Boyhood

In *The Pavilion,* Stark Young has recounted fully the story of his life until he was twenty-one, as he remembered it when a man of more than seventy. Although his account may have been affected by a lapse of years, it must always serve as the major source of information about his boyhood, though occasionally it can be corroborated and even supplemented by material from his letters and the memories of relatives and those who knew him. Artistically shaped but basically truthful, the volume records both the joys and the bitternesses of a Como boyhood in the 1880s and 1890s. Among the more joyful moments, Young mentions his early school days, notable, he thought, more for the discipline and the pious, moral sermonizing of the teachers than for actual educational experiences. He writes of his gift for mimicry, his pleasures in reading, and his interest in pictures of every sort. As a child, he was aware that his family was always troubled in their minds about the race question. More vivid than his memories of his education is his account of his delight in listening to the conversations of his aunts and uncles during the long Sunday afternoons on his uncle's front porch. Often Young accompanied his father in the horse-drawn buggy as he visited a sick or dying Negro in a distant cabin or a white patient in an isolated farmhouse. Young was disappointed when his father refused to permit him to take drawing lessons for fear that his son might become a professional artist. Dr. Young also insisted that the boy not be taught to work with a hammer and saw, because he knew that the temptation to stop school to help with family finances had prevented many a boy in small Southern towns from continuing his education through high school and beyond.

Long after Stark Young left Como, his teachers remembered him as an extraordinary child whose affection, intelligence, and receptiveness notably distinguished him from other children. Young's mental quickness, his interest in the meanings of words, and his immediate perception of ideas were prominent characteristics even in the lower grades. His two aunts, who lived in the household during his earliest years and knew him almost as well as did his mother, recalled his shyness and emotional sensitivity. They remembered his unusually intense affection for his sister Julia; but even more vividly they remarked upon his fervent devotion to his mother. Aware of Mollie Young's idolization of her little boy, they, and others, noticed his almost too remarkable love for her, an affection that seems to have reached the stage of a frantic dependence upon her. If there were perhaps something abnormal about this bond between mother and son, the aunts, if they were aware of it, as is unlikely, said nothing.

After the birth of her third child, Mrs. Young's health declined visibly. Dr. Young took his family, including Mollie's two sisters, to Florida for two years in an effort to bring about his wife's recovery; but her condition, perhaps either consumption or lung cancer, did not improve. She died early in the morning of 4 April 1890, while Stark Young was still in his eighth year. As an old man, he could still remember her last moments, his trip to the cemetery with his father to direct the gravediggers, and his impatience at his father's willingness to stop to talk with friends about her illness. In his autobiography, Young wrote that until he was almost twenty he could not bear to mention her name. Her death was the most grievous "wound" of his childhood. Although one can speculate about the causes of Young's sexual attitudes, the extraordinary bond of affection between him and his mother may have been a contributing factor. His life and that of his sister were radically altered by her death.

Stark Young's "Uncle Hugh" and his wife "Aunt Julia" took the children. Intermittently, between teaching positions, Mollie Young's sisters, Frances and Sarah, lived with the McGehees; and later Julia went to school wherever they happened to be teaching. They would spend the remainder of their lives with either Stark or Julia. Meanwhile, Stark Young continued his schooling in Como. Dr. Young's income, never very substantial, seems to have diminished to the point where he felt compelled to seek a larger practice in Memphis. In 1895 he found a position in Oxford as the associate of an established physician. In a very short time, he met and married Lydia Lewis Walton, recently widowed and the mother of two children. Dr. Young at once moved his family to Oxford. In the house of their stepmother, Stark and Julia were not happy. Stark lived there, however, while attending a "female academy" in Oxford as a day student before enrolling in 1896 as a special student at the University of Mississippi; and throughout the remainder of his student days, he continued to live at home. In 1897 he became a regularly enrolled freshman at the university.

Higher Education

At the University of Mississippi, Young was a good student in courses that emphasized English literature, Latin, Greek, and history, along with the required studies in science and mathematics. He took several courses in Shakespeare and English poetry from Professor Sarah McGehee Isom, who had acquired an international reputation as a teacher of elocution. From her Young acquired his initial enthusiasm for the theatre. During his first year at the university, he and a group of his friends produced a number of short plays, some out of old issues of *Godey's Lady's Book* and others written by Young himself, on an improvised stage in front of a house in the country belonging to his stepmother's mother. He joined his father's fraternity, Sigma Chi, and a literary society. He wrote poetry, acted in Shakespearean plays under Miss Isom's direction, and edited the student annual. He was graduated in 1901. Young's verdict upon this education, rendered years later in *The Pavilion,* was that it was not very solid or thorough, that it was not so scientific as it might have been in other institutions, but that it inculcated a great respect for the accomplishments of the past and rested upon something "that was honorable and high" (159). Perhaps one of the marks of this education was that in the year after he finished at the university Young read the Greek plays in Greek. Whatever its deficiencies, it gave Young a profound respect and enthusiasm for learning that remained with him throughout his life.

Aided by the financial support of his father and monthly checks from his two aunts, in the fall of 1901 Stark Young enrolled as a graduate student in English at Columbia University. Because of a coterie of brilliant professors, the Columbia English Department was widely recognized as perhaps the finest in the country. On its staff were such nationally known scholars as Brander Matthews, George Edward Woodberry, George Rice Carpenter, and William P. Trent. Most of these men were Southerners and almost all were directly concerned with the theatre. The department was especially well situated for study in the drama because of its immediate access to Broadway productions which could be, and often were, used in the classroom as practical demonstrations of theatre problems and critical theories. Brander Matthews, under whom Young concentrated his studies, was then considered the foremost theatre critic in America.

Matthews encouraged his students to follow closely the new and repertory plays of the current theatrical season. Young seems eagerly to have followed the advice. He saw, for example, Maude Adams in Barrie's *Quality Street,* Mrs. Patrick Campbell in *The Second Mrs. Tanqueray,* and Eleonora Duse in D'Annunzio's *La Gioconda, La Citta Morta,* and *Francesca Da Rimini.* He also saw performances by E. H. Sothern, John Drew, Lionel Barrymore, Otis Skinner, Annie Russell, Julia Marlowe, Mrs. Leslie Carter, and Mrs. Minnie Madern Fiske. With Matthews's approval, Young enjoyed the burlesques of Broadway productions staged by the remarkable company of Weber and Fields, whom Matthews called the American Aristophanes. Of course, Young attended these productions with no thought that one day he would find the experiences an invaluable source of material for his work as a professional drama critic. As one would expect, however, the bulk of his courses were concentrated in the standard English authors and the Greek and Roman classics. His thesis was a critique of the life and work of James Montgomery, the romantic poet and hymnodist, a contemporary of Wordsworth. In June 1902 Young was awarded the Master of Arts degree from Columbia.

Although his graduate study at Columbia had prepared him to teach English literature, Young felt no immediate inclination to pursue an academic career. After a few weeks' visit to Mississippi, he returned to New York and obtained a job as a reporter for a newspaper; but he soon found that he possessed little talent for journalism. For reasons not altogether clear—Young once intimated that he wished to wash out the taste of James Montgomery's banal verse—he left New York and rented a room in a boardinghouse near Canton, North Carolina. During the late winter months and spring of 1903, he read a great deal of English romantic poetry, Shakespeare and other Renaissance dramatists, Malory, Molière, Virgil, and Catullus. After he moved into a nearby cabin, he read Dante's *The Divine Comedy* with the aid of a literal translation and an Italian dictionary, often memorizing the Italian verses after he had worked out the sense of the passages. In later years, when Young had learned to read Italian with ease, he returned again and again to Dante (and the poetry of Leopardi) for inspiration and, at times, solace. From this experience in the North Carolina mountains dates his lifelong fondness for Italian literature, sculpture, and drama.

The months of study in North Carolina intensified Young's

commitment to literature. Had he been asked about his future plans, Young would probably have replied that he wanted more than anything else to write poetry. While a student at the University of Mississippi and at Columbia, he had published poetry in the *Ole Miss* annual and the *University of Mississippi Magazine*. In North Carolina, he wrote such poems as "Gordia" and "The Whippoorwill," which, like many of the other poems he had already published, he later revised for inclusion in *The Blind Man at the Window* (1906). During this time, he also completed a considerable portion of his poetic drama *Guenevere* (1906). The period had been fruitful both in terms of his writing and his education.

Young's talents and his formal education pointed him toward teaching. Years later, as he looked back upon his education, he was often inclined to speak disparagingly of his intellectual accomplishments. The fact is, however, that his education had given him a first-rate knowledge of the Greek and Latin classics, English poetry, and the drama, both classical and modern. He had read a great deal of history, and for a person of his background he had a remarkable grasp of the fine arts. Although he may have appeared to strangers as a bookish person, he was in no sense a pedant. His professors and friends at Columbia found his wit engaging and his conversation often brilliant. He already possessed the pleasing combination of learning and charm that enabled him to become an outstanding teacher and critic.

An opening on the faculty of a small military school at Water Valley, a railroad center just south of Oxford, provided a chance for Young to begin teaching, continue his writing, and live in Mississippi near his father and sister. In April 1904 the spring session of the school was cut short because of an outbreak of smallpox. Young returned to Oxford, and early in June 1904, he accepted a position on the faculty of the University of Mississippi as "assistant in English." His plans for the coming year settled, he left at once for a summer abroad.

By the middle of June, Young was in Italy. On the ship he had improved his knowledge of Italian until he could, as he said, "jabber" with almost any Italian he met and even swear at the cabmen. From Naples he went immediately to Rome to realize a childhood ambition to see the Forum, the palaces of the Caesars, the arches of triumph, and St. Peter's. Young spent most of the summer in Italy, visiting, besides Rome and Naples, Florence, Milan, and Venice. Leaving Italy, he spent the remainder of the summer in England, where he acquired a firsthand knowledge of the places associated with the Arthurian legends and the English romantic poets. He would make good use of these experiences in his lectures on English literature, in his poetry, and in *Guenevere.* Of all the travels abroad he would make in later years, this first visit to the two countries for whose literature he had the greatest admiration was probably the most exciting. He was making his own Grand Tour. Back in Oxford, he began his career as a college professor.

Chapter Two

Academia

In the fall of 1904, when Stark Young became a professor at the University of Mississippi, he entered upon an academic career that for the next seventeen years would be brilliantly successful. He would teach in succession at the University of Mississippi, the University of Texas, Dartmouth College, and Amherst College. At each institution he would make a distinct, highly individual contribution; and everywhere he would be popular with both students and colleagues, in the classroom enthusiastic but demanding, and on campus witty and charming. Long after they had taken his courses, students remembered his emphasis upon language, an emphasis that included an insistence upon the selection of the precise word to convey a meaning, the felicitous turn of phrase, and the development of a literary style. Under him, "rhetoric," as English composition courses were then called, became an exciting experience, and courses in literature pointed the student toward the development of his own intellectual and artistic potential. Among colleagues who themselves were teachers of acknowledged ability, Young stood out as an academic "star."

At the University of Mississippi

Ever since his student days at the university, Young had contributed poetry to the *Ole Miss* annuals. Between 1900 and 1905 he published nine poems, including "At Eventide," "The Song of the Night-Blooming Jasmine," "Last Leaves," "Reaper's Song," "To My Lady Sleeping," "To a Little Blue-Flower in Cornwall," and several poems entitled "Song." During approximately the same period, eleven of his poems appeared in the *University of Mississippi Magazine,* including "Song of Peleas to Melisande," "Ballade of the Round Table," "Casement Song," "Night and Love," "Moonrise," "Spring Song," several sonnets, and the topical poem "Ode in Mississippi's Troubled Hour."

Virtually all of these poems were reprinted, after revision, in *The Blind Man at the Window,* published late in 1906, Young's final year in Mississippi.[1] The thin volume, bound in green, contains sixty poems, the longest ("Gordia") of 231 lines and the shortest ("Last Leaves") of six. Young employed a number of verse forms and rhyme schemes: sonnets, ballads, odes, couplets, blank verse, and triolets. Although he made no structural divisions in the book, the poems may be conveniently divided into several groups with, of course, some overlapping: nature poems, verses that reflect his reading, and poetry that is inspired by Young's personal relationships.

Fifteen of the shorter poems, several of which are entitled merely "Song," stem from Young's response to nature. For the most part, a general tone of autumnal sadness and melancholy pervades these nature lyrics. Among the best examples are "Whippoorwill," "Spring Song," "Sunset Song," "Swallows," "The Little Garden," "Nocturne," and "Song" ("White rain and green fields"). Although Young's verses have a freshness and originality, the influence of Burns, Wordsworth, and Tennyson may readily be seen. Young's "To a Mouse," in fact, may have been written intentionally to recall Burns's poem of the same title, while "Last Leaves" makes the same point that Tennyson makes in "Crossing the Bar." Even more directly, Young's "Swallows" reminds the reader of Tennyson's "Flower in the Crannied Wall."

In the poems that reflect his reading of Malory's and Tennyson's treatments of the Arthurian legends, Young combines the note of sadness dominant in his nature poems with his criticism of the present. In such poems as the "Ballad of the Round Table," "To a Little Blue-Flower in Cornwall," and "Lines Written at Tintagel in King Arthur's Country," the young poet looks back admiringly upon the courage, nobility, and religious faith found among the knights of the Round Table but lacking in modern times. In "The Seekers," a product of Young's study of Dante, the poet envisions himself walking along the shore of hell and encountering various unhappy individuals who are vainly trying to find God through human reason. In "The Dead Shore," an even more Dantesque poem than "The Seekers," a hooded figure suggesting Virgil leads the poet along the desert shore of a lightless sea, where he views hordes of sinners struggling to find ultimate answers to the mysteries of death and eternity. The religious motif is continued in the dramatic monologue (in the form of a letter) "Abner the Nazarene, to Caesar Linius Caecilius Secundus, Propraetor of Pontus," in which Young depicts the anguish of an early Christian who has denied Christ but can find no peace until he has abrogated his oath and voiced his faith. The poem recalls Browning's "An Epistle, Containing the Strange Medical Experience of Karshish, the Arab Physician."

"The Return" reflects Young's fondness for Tennyson's handling of classical themes. Dedicated to Alexander L. Bondurant, Young's professor of Latin at the University of Mississippi, it recounts the story of Ulysses' return and his faith in the constancy of Penelope. Although it deals with a classical and literary theme, the poem belongs to Young's love lyrics and should be placed with his "Orpheus" and "Gordia," the lovely maiden who died for the love of Prosper.

The most original of the poems in *The Blind Man at the Window* are those whose source lies in Young's personal experience. The sonnet "To My Sister" is a tender expression of his love for Julia McGehee Young. Even more personal to Young are the two poems that deal with his memories of his mother, "The Mother" and "Written at My Mother's Grave." In the former, the mother recalls rocking her dead baby while she herself lies dying. In the latter, Young writes directly of his own mother and remembers incidents of childhood, memories that are still "green and fresh and pure" (37). The intensity of his emotion is apparent in the poem, perhaps the most successful piece in the volume.

The "Ode in Mississippi's Troubled Hour" (23–28), which Young read before the alumni society of the University of Mississippi in June 1904, is unique in the volume, since it is essentially a topical poem dealing with racial issues. Early in the ode, Young depicts Mississippi as a land where, despite good harvests of cotton and corn, the cry of "Woe, ah, woe" is heard again and again. Crimes are committed, women are not safe from rape, and "mobs and violence . . . Increase and lessen not with passing time." The "outside hand" has stirred racial strife and now calls for racial equality. Young's answer is that the racial problem is "our own" and that "the negro must be raised as God sees fit" in the "gradual long working-out" of God's plan. Mississippi (and the South) is seen as God's tool: "And though the South must bear the Afric scourge, / The chastisement may leave her yet more fair. . . ." The poem, though not in keeping with the other pieces in the volume, is significant as the earliest expression of Young's attitude toward racial matters in the South.

The most ambitious poem in *The Blind Man at the Window* gives title to the work. It is preceded by a sonnet, "I saw a blind man at his window sitting." In the octave of this sonnet, the blind man is represented as being aware of the beauty of the evening from the sounds of the birds and wind. In the sestet, the poet concludes that like the blind man "we," eager but blind, watch from the "shadowed chamber of our life" (39) and seek to experience reality through imperfect senses. This sonnet and the succeeding one, which develops a similar idea, serve as a prelude to the title poem that follows.

Although "The Blind Man at the Window" (40–42) is divided into two parts—"Morning-Joy" and "Evening-Contemplation"—both deal with the same theme. For Young, all senses are but "poor channels" to an "inner eye" that has a deeper vision of the "divine harmony" and "glimmerings / Beyond this life, wherein we grope in sleep, / Stumbling in dreams toward the Great Light." The poem contains a good deal of involved syntax, and in places its meaning is obscure; nevertheless, it may be taken as a statement of Young's poetic faith.

Young was probably pleased with the reception given his initial volume of poetry. In the South, it was particularly well received. He was often compared to Sidney Lanier, one reviewer remarking that "never since Lanier . . . has such poetry been written."[2] Other critics, while noting instances of his imitation of other poets, conceded his originality and emphasized the promise these poems held for his future career. Except for the verse drama *Guenevere*,[3] published about the same time as *The Blind Man at the Window,* and a few other poems that appeared in magazines, Young did little to fulfill this prediction; rather, he turned his artistic talents into other directions.

Guenevere, however, marks a shift in Young's interest from short lyrical poems to the drama and a much more ambitious effort than anything he had written earlier. Although he knew Tennyson's "Guinevere" in the *Idylls of the King,* his primary source is Malory's *Morte d'Arthur.* Young had probably not read Richard Hovey's *Launcelot and Guenevere: A Poem in Dramas* (1891); nor did he know Ernest Rhys's *Guenevere* (1905) or Graham Hill's tragedy *Guinevere* (1906). In making the story into a drama, Young worked without specific models.

Although Mordred's plot to capture Guenevere, betray her and Launcelot to King Arthur, and in the ensuing chaos seize the kingdom forms the political background of the plan and occupies much of the first two acts, Young clearly intended to subordinate this material to the analysis of the queen's feelings toward Arthur and Launcelot. In the third act, she is placed on trial before Arthur in the great council hall. She defends herself by explaining that she has loved them both "but differently." Of Arthur she says: "Since thou'rt ideal, they that love thee love / Thee as a mystic symbol, or a bodied / Soul of some dear thing, not as frail man." She concludes that "thy kingdom is thy spouse . . . not I." She has loved Launcelot as a man who lives in the world, as a soldier and as a lover. She will give up Launcelot, retire from the world, and live with the sisters in the convent by Boscastle. As she leaves the hall, she unmasks Mordred and calls him a traitor.

The final two acts take place in the convent by Boscastle. In act 4, Guenevere is about to take her vows but hesitates, uncertain whether she has really given up Camelot. She recalls that while the "dreaming king" forgot her, Launcelot loved her and she loved him. The queen fears that she may renounce the world and yet lose her heaven, "be neither / Spiritual nor fleshly, saint nor queen." As Arthur bids her farewell, he admits equal guilt with her: she with her love for Launcelot and he with "seeing men not as men but as symbols vague. / Stargazing I did lose the earthly road." As a disillusioned idealist, Arthur cannot respond to her affirmation of the good in life. When he leaves, she rushes out to plead with him to take her back to Camelot. Returning to the convent, she cries out that she has now lost both kingdoms.

The last act takes place a year later. Arthur has been slain, and Camelot is but a "den of plots and arms." Guenevere is dying. Launcelot has come to take her to France with him; but Guenevere refuses to go, denying him even one final kiss. He declares that he will go to a hermitage and pray for them. As her last request, she asks him to take her body to Glastonbury for burial near Arthur; and as she dies, the sounds of the knights returning from Camelot, where the new king, Constantine, has been crowned, are heard outside. In the final brief scene, without dialogue, Launcelot and his seven knights are seen carrying the queen's bier on their shoulders in a wood near Glastonbury.

Young's *Guenevere,* though apprentice work, is a creditable effort. He perceived that the dramatically effective portions of Malory's story are the trial of the queen and her farewell scenes with Arthur and Launcelot. In the presentation of this material, he made his most original contribution. He was less successful in making Guenevere an appealing heroine embodying a conflict between the flesh and the spirit. In evaluating the play, however, one must remember that the essential actions, the final outcome, and the presentation of the characters were to a considerable degree restricted by the basic story in Malory. *Guenevere* was an ambitious venture, perhaps too ambitious for Young at this stage in his career.

While teaching at the University of Mississippi, Young was involved in other dramatic ventures. He wrote and probably directed several one-act plays, and he served as an assistant to Miss Sarah McGehee Isom, professor of elocution. During the spring semester, Miss Isom usually directed her students in a dramatic presentation, sometimes dramatic readings and on other occasions the acting of a Shakespearean play. Early in 1904, while teaching at Water Valley, Young had written the prologue for her production of Shakespeare's *Julius Caesar.* After her death on 29 April 1905, Young began to direct the student performances. On 27 April 1907 the University Players, under his direction, produced Richard Brinsley Sheridan's *The Rivals* at the Oxford Opera House, a performance reviewed enthusiastically in the *Oxford Eagle.*

At the University of Texas

Young declined to teach in the following summer school session because he wished to spend the summer, as he had the year before, in Italy studying Dante. He returned in time to begin teaching in the fall semester, but early in October he was unexpectedly offered a newly created position on the faculty of the University of Texas; and by the middle of the month he had resigned and was on his way to Austin. Young's colleagues viewed his departure with considerable regret, though they were glad for his promotion in rank and salary. At a special meeting, the university faculty expressed appreciation of his teaching and "the high esteem in which we hold Mr. Young for his genial spirit, his sincerity of character, and his uprightness as a man."[4]

For the next eight years, Stark Young taught courses in writing and English literature at the University of Texas. Regularly he spent the summers in Europe, more often than not in Italy. He lived for weeks at a time in Florence or Rome. He made friends with Italian scholars in monasteries and sought their help in studying Dante. He made brief visits to Venice, Naples, Milan, and other Italian cities. During one summer, he lived in Greece; and he often stopped in England on the way to and from Italy. Back at the university, he enlivened his lectures with references to the art and literature he had studied abroad.

Young's enthusiasm for the fine arts and determination to succeed on his own as a creative artist helped to make him a popular teacher. His classes attracted large numbers of students, and he was in constant demand as a speaker. In addition to teaching writing or rhetoric, Young offered as his most advanced courses two year-long studies of the development of the drama from its beginnings in ancient Greece. He alternated a two-semester sequence dealing with tragedy and a year's course in comedy. Young strongly believed that English professors should also be creative writers, an attitude by no means shared by all of his colleagues. To understand fully the complexities of poetry, he thought, one must write poetry; to teach a novel well, one should have at least attempted to write one (before he left Mississippi Young had begun a novel about Southern life but failed to finish it); to be most effective as a drama teacher, one must have written plays. Soon after joining the Texas faculty, he startled the Fortnightly Club, a research society devoted to the humanities, by substituting for the usual research paper a reading of his own one-act play "Madretta."

Early in the fall of 1908, editorials—possibly inspired by Stark Young—in the student newspaper, the *Texan,* advocated the formation of a Masque and Wig club at the university. Responding with enthusiasm to the proposal, Young invited the editor and an engineering student to discuss the project at his residence. Although little was accomplished, he revived the matter after the Christmas holidays. At a meeting on 7 January 1909, Young and fifteen students held an organizational meeting. They selected the name Curtain Club and agreed that the purpose of the club would be "to stimulate the study of modern plays by reading, and to stimulate the study of plays of the early English stage by acting."[5] Stark Young was chosen "conductor"; later he would be called "coach" and then "director." The group also determined that membership would be limited to twenty, women would be excluded, and the first play to be staged would be Ben Jonson's *Epicoene, or the Silent Woman,* on 27 February 1909. Reflecting upon the inception of the club, one of the original members wrote later: "Above it all hovered the spirit of Stark Young. Without such a genius there would have been no Curtain Club. . . . His artistic blending, his religion of beauty dominated things that had to do with the Curtain Club. Curtain Club is another way of spelling Stark Young."[6]

In less than six weeks, Young had selected the cast, taught the students how to act and speak their lines, designed attractive sets, and obtained costumes for the performance of *Epicoene.* The production was an instant success. On opening night, President Mezes, most of the faculty, students, and prominent citizens of Austin applauded enthusiastically. The high artistic quality of the production, especially Young's attention to minute detail, established a level of excellence that characterized all of the succeeding plays given under Young's direction.

Although the Curtain Club encouraged its members to read a wide field of plays, tragedies as well as comedies, Young thought that students could perform best in comedy. He staged one major play each year. In 1910 the play was Beaumont and Fletcher's *The Knight of the Burning Pestle;* in 1911, Molière's *L'Avare* (*The Miser*); in 1912, Goldoni's *Il ventaglio* (*The Fan*); in 1913, Regnard's *Le legataire universel* (*The Sole Heir*); in 1914, Porter's *The Two Angry Women of Abington;* and in 1915, Gogol's *Revisor or the Inspector General* (presented with Young's adaptation of Leacock's burlesque *Behind the Beyond*)—the last production under Young's direction. The texts of the foreign plays acted by the Curtain Club were translations made by Stark Young. On Halloween, 1909, he produced *Beelzebubble,* a farce that he had written to please the club members as well as the audience.

The success of the Curtain Club's productions led to invitations to take the company on tour throughout the state. By the time Young left the university in 1916, the Curtain Club was offering performances in Austin, Dallas, Houston, Denton, Sherman, San Marcos, and other Texas cities. Its road tours were limited only by the time which the faculty permitted students to be absent from the campus. The performances of the club on tour were thought to have stimulated interest in dramatic productions of little theatre groups throughout the Southwest.

Young's work with the Curtain Club not only gave him valuable practical experience in directing but also familiarized him with all aspects of play production. His artistic talents included a self-taught but remarkable skill in sketching and painting, abilities that he now used to great advantage. As Howard Mumford Jones, a subsequent director of the Curtain Club, later recalled, Young "displayed marked and original ability"[7] in designing scenic effects and costumes. The training of young boys to act female roles convincingly was a tribute to Young's understanding of acting. He worked with little or no special equipment and produced his plays in auditoriums or halls that lacked even the most primitive facilities for staging theatrical performances.

In teaching students, Young emphasized the importance of method. By method, he meant, as an original member of the Curtain Club explained, "the study of the school of acting and interpretation to which the play belongs; [it] . . . implies development in range of taste and style, and in breadth of understanding."[8] For example, Young taught that *Epicoene* should be acted "in the style of the comedy of manners, but English in tone rather than French." *The Knight of the Burning Pestle* was "pure burlesque," while *The Fan* was a comedy of intrigue. The careful study of method involved "a minute attention to details which has been the source of the Club's greatest and finest influence . . . expressed in acquaintance with several schools of acting, and in a new appreciation of histrionic art."[9]

As a result of the Curtain Club productions, Stark Young established himself nationally as a leader of amateur play productions. After he left the university, the Curtain Club continued to perform successfully under a number of outstanding directors. The next year women were admitted to membership and female roles henceforth were played by women. In 1916 Young was succeeded by William L. Sowers and in 1919 by Howard Mumford Jones, under whose direction the Club continued to stage outstanding productions of notable plays.

While directing the activities of the Curtain Club, Young was also writing plays and drama criticism. In 1911 he began to write for the *Drama,* a recently founded periodical devoted to the theatre and published in Chicago. For it he wrote several articles; in the most important of them, he urged playwrights to develop a method in drama that would combine "actuality, inner significance, and expression."[10] Early in the following year, he became one of the magazine's contributing editors and a member of its advisory board, which included Professor George P. Baker of Harvard and Young's former professor at Columbia, Brander Matthews. Meanwhile, Young was writing one-act plays, and in May 1912 the student newspaper announced that seven of his pieces had been accepted for publication in the *Drama.*[11] Although not published in the magazine, the seven plays appeared under the title *Addio, Madretta and Other Plays.*[12] The works included in the attractive, dark-green volume with gold lettering were *Addio, Madretta, The Star in the Trees, The Twilight Saint, The Dead Poet, The Seven Kings and the Wind,* and *The Queen of Sheba.*

In the history of American drama, particularly the short play, Stark Young's seven pieces represent an important contribution. One-act plays, of course, were not new. Traditionally, they had been used as introductory to the main dramatic performance and upon occasion as afterpieces. In the late nineteenth century, Augustus Thomas and Clyde Fitch had written in the form; but the most popular writer had been William Dean Howells. Although his work could be, and was, acted upon the stage, most persons knew his plays through their publication in the *Atlantic Monthly* and *Harper's Magazine.* Brander Matthews, whose work Stark Young certainly knew, had also published a number of brief dramatic pieces.

About 1911, however, the astonishing rise of the Little The-
atre movement began to take place. Manifestations of popular
interest in dramatics can be seen in the organization of the
Drama League (1910), the Wisconsin Players (1911), the Toy
Theatre of Boston (1912), the Chicago Little Theatre (1912),
and George Pierce Baker's "47 Workshop" theatre (1912).
Young was a leader in this movement. Even before it began,
he wrote his seven brilliantly conceived short plays, and in the
Curtain Club he anticipated by three years much that George
Pierce Baker would endeavor to accomplish in his "47 Workshop." Although the one-act play would be largely confined
to amateur productions in little theatres and universities—except
occasionally, as in Noel Coward's *Tonight at 8:30*, the form
would never be popular on Broadway—out of the short play
movement that Young and Baker were encouraging would arise
the Washington Square Players and later the Provincetown Players with whom Stark Young would be associated. From them
and others one can trace the rise of the modern American theatre.

The first two plays in *Addio, Madretta and Other Plays* present
basically the same situation. In *Addio* ("Good-bye"), Susa, a
Sicilian girl, has been separated by gossip from her lover and
come to New Orleans, where she has found a new friend, Harry
Boyd. They have arranged to meet in a bakery shop kept by
a German immigrant. By coincidence, Tomasso, an organ
grinder, is in the shop. He too has been separated from his
sweetheart and has spent the past two years looking for her.
He is a pathetic figure, lame, poor, and saddened by the death
of his pet monkey. As Susa and Tomasso converse, they tacitly
recognize each other. But Tomasso abandons his claim to Susa
in favor of the young, healthy Harry; and Susa, though torn
between the two men, leaves the shop with Harry. Her decision
is the crucial point in the play. In *Madretta*, Young also deals
with a triangular situation. Nani, a French girl, has married
Simon, a foreman on the levee. Their baby Pierre has died
and their marriage has been strained. While he is away at work,
Jean Mari endeavors to seduce Nani, whom Simon calls Madretta
("little mother"), by offering to take her back to New Orleans.
As Madretta is packing to leave with Jean, Simon returns unexpectedly because a break in the levee threatens an approaching

flood. He encounters Jean, and in the fight that ensues Simon receives a fatal wound. Madretta must decide between escaping with Jean or remaining to comfort the dying Simon and perishing herself in the flood. She chooses to remain with Simon. Although the decisions of both women, Susa and Madretta, stem from their characters, Madretta's loyalty is more appealing than Susa's selfishness.

In many respects, these two plays are similar. The audience witnesses a crisis in the lives of three persons who are vividly defined in terms of background, appearance, vocation, nationality, and mental outlook. Although the plays begin at the "fifth act," Young provides ample information for the playgoer to infer the pertinent information about the dramatis personae. In both plays, a woman must decide between two radically different men; and the choice she makes arises from her own character and those of her lovers. Each work is a highly unified composition, every word and phrase contributing to the total effect. Produced according to the explicit and detailed stage directions, these realistic short pieces in prose make effective theatre within the reach of amateur actors.

In *Addio, Madretta and Other Plays,* Young was seeking to formulate his ideas about dramatic styles. He worked with a fine discriminating grasp of dramatic tradition from the Greeks to his own century. In writing *Addio* and *Madretta,* he responded to the realistic dramas of August Strindberg and Henrik Ibsen. In Young's words, these plays were meant to reproduce life as it is, to photograph "the exterior manifestations of life," and to leave to the imagination whatever was not expressed in words or acts. *Addio* and *Madretta* are largely confined to situations and problems easily understood through speech. In these realistic dramas, Young believed, the playwright emphasized "the particular manifestation rather than the idea, the phenomenon rather than its eternal content and application."[13] In other plays in this volume and later, as a drama critic for the *New Republic,* he would take a different view.

In their reliance upon symbol, fantasy, metaphor, and psychological analysis, the other five plays in the volume owe something to the short plays of Maurice Maeterlinck and his followers. The air of unreality of Young's pieces is heightened by the settings, lighting, stage effects, and, especially, the poetry.

Young felt that poetry was more suitable than prose for plays that seek to express the ideal and are removed "in time and place from the actual as it exists for us." He stressed the value of music to the Greek dramatist. Music, he thought, added an emotional quality that assisted one's intellectual faculties to grasp the utmost significance of the idea being conveyed. As Young said, "the word behind the music defines the emotion, gives point to the general idea expressed." His argument is well summarized in his statement: "Wagner has reached thousands to whom Ibsen is still an alien." The modern dramatist, however, must leave music to the opera; but he may still use poetry to help him reveal truth and to arouse the audience to receive it "with all our faculties, imagination, enthusiasm, delight or despair, as well as with bare reason."[14] In his later drama criticism, Young continued to value the poetic, mystical, imaginative aspects of dramatic style. In reviewing a performance of Maeterlinck's *Pelléas and Mélisande* in 1923, for example, Young praised the play for achieving "no little of the wonder and mystery from which art as well as science springs." Although he did not believe this play was a great drama, he felt that it threw off "constant suggestions of beautiful things," not the least of which was a "belief in the beautiful and the poetic." The successful actor, he wrote, must have a "poetic understanding" of a drama.[15]

Throughout Young's plays, the primary theme is the role of art and the artist, a role that is never sharply defined but is suggested through metaphor or myth and symbol. *The Star in the Trees* contains a warning to the artist (and everyman) against escaping from the world of reality into the realm of the unreal, here faeryland (in *The Queen of Sheba*, it is imagination or madness). In *The Star in the Trees*, Astorri and Lyane, brother and sister, at twilight seek to enter faeryland to find happiness and "dim oblivion from life and grief" (64). But they find the inhabitants of the magic wood, Dew, the water nymph, the Night Wind, Echo, Daphne, and Syrinz, desire passionately to return to the flesh so that they may die and forget their sorrows. Despite their testimony, the Queen of Faerie promises Astorri a lotus land of forgetfulness in which the affairs of men, pain, and death touch them not. She will make him forget "the world of time and grief " (61) and become a brother to the tree and star (nature?). Just as the Queen is about to slit his eyes to blind him to the world forever, Lyane cries out to God to show a sign; at once a burning cross appears in the aspen tree, and the Queen of Faerie vanishes. The Voice of the Aspen Tree tells Astorri to turn back to life, not to leave it, and find his land of faery in the love of his fellowmen. As the arms of the cross dwindle to a star, the Voice commands: "Follow the star" which Lyane calls "Christ" (64).

In *The Twilight Saint,* Young again phrases his attitude toward the artist in religious terms. In this play, perhaps the least dramatic piece in the collection, the poet Guido seeks worldly fame through his art. He complains bitterly that the necessity of nursing his wife Lisetta, who has been ill for months, keeps him from realizing his ambitions. For her part, Lisetta sorrows that she is keeping him from his writing. St. Francis of Assisi comforts her by explaining that "love is all thou owest / For service unto God and thy Beloved" (79). When Guido meets St. Francis, he teaches that God "Hath given thee thy soul for its own life, / And not for glory among men" (87). And Guido realizes that in Lisetta he has his glory, "Thou art my saint and shrine!" (11). To become a great poet, the artist must renounce self-glory and learn the self-effacing joy of love.

In *The Dead Poet,* Young deals with the permanence of art and the solace it can bring to the living. Again, the setting is a wood at twilight. Alleene is walking with her Mother and Father, and all three are disconsolate over the death of the poet whom they have loved. As the parents determine to return home—"Our son is dead, there is no hope of solace" (95)—the Blind Child tells them that he has spoken with the dead poet. "Have ye not heard his voice along the grass?" (97), asks the Blind Child. "He is as one with the Eternal Heart" (98). When the Father cannot understand the Child's meaning, he tells them to return home in hope, for "The festal lamp will shine for thee again" (99). The "high gods" of Greece are not dead is the message carried by the Wind. The poet, though dead, lives through his poetry, and his vision has descended to the Child, who paradoxically though blind is a "seer." If not possessed by the Child's confident vision, Alleene and

her parents return home comforted by the Child's promise to
be with them "and he with me" (102). Art, poetry, the high
gods of Greece, live eternally through the poet, and, perhaps,
the Blind Child may yet become a poet himself.

The characterization in the preceding short plays is extremely
slight, since the characters stand primarily for ideas. In *The Seven
Kings and the Wind,* Young offers even less stress upon character.
This play is actually a dramatic poem concerned with seven
theories of art and its function. The setting is a chamber in an
unidentified palace. Seven kings stand by a window; outside it
is "black night." They are waiting for the coming of the king
(the divine Wind). Each of the assembled kings expresses his
temperament: the optimist (Felix), the idealistic philosopher
(Platon), the materialist (Astamore), the East (a dreamer), the
West (militant), the North (mystical and tender), and the South
(classic and definite). Each king reports what he sees outside
the window in terms of his philosophy as dawn begins to light
the horizon. All agree that the glass must be broken for them
to see clearly their vision, an act that symbolizes the expansion
of the setting from the palace room to the universe. When
the glass is broken, the Wind rushes in, and the kings fall on
their knees. A Voice in the Wind concludes the play: "He is
so much as thou dost apprehend, / The rest for thee is but
the Universe" (116). In other words, each individual must respond to art (the divine) in his own way, and he apprehends
only so much of it as his vision permits.

Of the plays in this volume, the final drama, *The Queen of
Sheba,* is the most original conception, the most moving expression of an idea, and the best unified. The single setting is a
Gothic chamber, representing a king's harem with pictures of
women, prints, paintings, and magazine covers spotted around
the walls. In reality the chamber is a madhouse. There are four
characters. Adelle and Auvergne are lovers and cousins. Adelle
explains that in his youth Auvergne sought wisdom and in following the "cloudy heights of thought" (130) snapped the chord
that bound him to reality. "Reason the traitor failed him in
his need" (130), she says. In his madness, Auvergne thinks
himself King Solomon and Adelle the Queen of Sheba. Adelle
has also become mad and believes she is the Queen of Sheba.
With them is the humble, ugly Gawain, born insane, who chroni-

cles the progress of Auvergne's fatal illness and his death. The three are attended by a Sister who provides a minimum of exposition for the audience.

As the play opens, Auvergne as King Solomon welcomes Adelle his Queen of Sheba. Beautiful to him as she is, he thinks she has recently appeared strange. She admits that at times she has looked at him and found all his glory "mocked and made hideous" (124). Auvergne laments that "in this world men know not true from false" (126). Suddenly, Adelle cries out and turns away; her madness has vanished and she looks upon Auvergne not as King Solomon but as a madman. As she tears away her veil and costume, Auvergne views her as a stranger.

Throughout act 2, Adelle is sane, though Auvergne remains mad. Without his Sheba, he lies in bed waiting for death. Talking with the Sister, Adelle questions the justice of God that upon Auvergne, who has "seen the glory of the world and drunk / The wine of dreams" (131), has fallen Doom and Death. The Sister replies that "God / Evens the scales of life" (130). Auvergne has also had his joys. To Adelle, Auvergne's plight is that of a man who has pursued wisdom or reason to the point where he has become "Wise Solomon, and is no more Auvergne" (131). She contrasts him with Gawain, who has never enjoyed reason, never lived, but entered life as dead. Hoping to save Auvergne, Adelle once more puts on her veil and costume as the Queen of Sheba, but Auvergne is already beyond hearing or seeing her.

In 1922 Young revised *The Queen of Sheba* and published it in *Theatre Arts*.[16] At that time he added the character of a young doctor to clarify the exposition. The Sister explains to the Doctor that Auvergne's father forbade Auvergne to marry Adelle because they were cousins and "there was already enough madness" (153) in the family. Auvergne, who became mad first, has been in the asylum for ten years and his parents are now dead. The Sister and the Doctor, who speak in prose, reflect upon the madness of the lovers. The Doctor concludes that "they have the freedom the soul dreams and shudders at" (154). For himself, he cannot "keep in my science, nor take this as a mere madness, when there is so much beauty and sorrow and glory" (158). Young has also expanded Adelle's role somewhat to emphasize the parallel and contrast she offers to Auvergne.

Near the end of the play, after she has regained her sanity, Adelle compares herself to him:

> And where am I,
> Who love his soul's height and sorrow,
> That are the same in him even now as ever
> But yet are made vain and lost?
> Where should I be but lost?
>
> (160)

Young felt that such additions helped to define the issues without substantially altering the meaning.

Although Adelle and Auvergne are lovers, the primary theme of *The Queen of Sheba* is not love. The central idea of the play relates to the artist's need for a balance between imagination and realism in the conduct of life. As Auvergne moves further and further into the realm of the imagination, he loses contact with reality. He reaches the point where he can love Adelle only when she exists in his imagination as the Queen of Sheba. When he sees her as she is, he finds her loathsome. Adelle undergoes a parallel experience but with a different outcome. At first, she too soars beyond reason into imagination (madness). Then, when she regains possession of her power to grasp reality, she finds Auvergne repulsive. But when she attains a measure of balance between the two positions, she can understand the beautiful in Auvergne and loves him. As applied to the artist, Young seems to imply that the artist must have his dreams and his glimpses of pure beauty, but he must also temper them with the reality of the suffering and pain of living.

Throughout his tenure at the University of Texas, Young sought to free himself from demands upon his time that seemed to prevent him from fulfilling his artistic ambitions. Each success of the Curtain Club, gratifying as it was, multiplied the time required to manage its affairs; and Young's popularity as a teacher added to the number of his students, thereby increasing the demands upon him for talking to students, reading term papers, and grading examinations. Despite the praise and his personal popularity, Young felt more and more that the faculty and the administration actually cared little about artistic matters.

As a "decent remonstrance against the miserable attitude that is creeping into this college" and an effort to express its "rather tottering humanism," Young determined to found a literary magazine.[17] As the result of his efforts, the first issue of the *Texas Review* appeared in June 1915. As editor, Young planned the journal along the lines of the *Yale Review* and invited his friends to contribute articles. The first issue contained a greeting by Edmund Gosse and contributions from Madison Cawein, Maurice Hewlett, Charlotte Wilson, Eunice Tietjens, Tucker Brooke, and Carl Van Doren—an impressive list and a testimony to Young's reputation. The second issue, published in September, featured contributions by such writers as Josephine Preston Peabody, William Peterfield Trent, John Erskine, Hobart C. Chatfield-Taylor, Alvin S. Johnson, Max Eastman, Julian Huxley, and Sir Gilbert Murray. From this number, which was to be Young's last as editor, Archibald Henderson's essay, "America and the Drama: A Forecast," had to be omitted; but it appeared in the next issue. Young's own contributions were "On Reeking of the Soil," in which he stated the editorial policy of the review, and "Poet Talk—Age Quod Agis," dealing with free verse.

The establishment of the *Texas Review,* however, did not quiet Young's restlessness. In the summer of 1915 he was invited to teach at Dartmouth College, and while there he negotiated with Alexander Meiklejohn, president of Amherst College, for a position on the Amherst faculty. Young accepted Meiklejohn's offer of a full professorship at a higher salary than Young was receiving at Texas, and in the fall of 1915 he moved to Amherst.

At Amherst College

From 1915 to 1921 Young taught at Amherst. His immediate popularity with students and faculty quickly dissipated his initial apprehension over teaching New England students in this small college town whose conservative population had once included Solomon Stoddard, Jonathan Edwards, and Emily Dickinson. The same combination of wit, personal charm, and sound scholarship that had been the basis of his appeal in Oxford and Austin proved equally successful at Amherst. Young worked to emphasize both literary appreciation and artistic creativity among the students. At his request, President Meiklejohn invited Robert Frost, then a virtually unknown poet whose work Young admired, to join the Amherst faculty. Frost's presence, however, did not turn out well for Young. Disliking Young's poetry and his liberal views, Frost soon became jealous of Young's popularity in and out of the classroom. He collected and circulated student gossip about Young's homosexuality and sought to have Meiklejohn discharge him on moral grounds. Meiklejohn refused, and Frost took the occasion to offer his resignation.

While at Amherst, Young found new outlets for his writing and made new friends. Alvin S. Johnson, a close friend and former colleague of Young at the University of Texas but now one of the editors of the recently founded *New Republic,* recommended Young to Herbert Croly, the editor in chief. In the summer of 1917 Croly, author of the influential *Promise of American Life* (1909), accepted five articles from Young. About this time, Young became acquainted with a number of persons prominently connected with the theatre, several of whom would become his close associates in the years to come. Such names as Robert Edmond Jones, Kenneth Macgowan, Eugene O'Neill, Jacob Ben-Ami, Eleonora Duse, and Alexander Woollcott appear frequently in Young's correspondence. In July 1919 Edith J. R. Isaacs, who became a devoted friend and enthusiastic admirer, published Young's one-act play *At the Shrine* in *Theatre Arts Magazine,* which she edited. Young's work was a subtly drawn, "fifth-act" study of the tension arising from the conflict between a priest and a prostitute over his nephew and her lover. Young's book reviews and essays also began to appear in the *Bookman, Nation, Dial,* and *Yale Review.* Although usually his contributions dealt with literary criticism, at times he wrote about art, religion, and drama. During the winter of 1919–20, while on leave from Amherst in Spain and Italy, Young sent back to *Theatre Arts Magazine* a series of articles about the foreign theatre. Increasingly, his work dealt with drama criticism, and by 1921, when he resigned from Amherst, he was virtually committed to writing about plays, acting, directing, and theatrical performances.

Young's resignation from Amherst was clearly a turning point in his career. Now almost forty, he had enjoyed a successful career at three major institutions as teacher, scholar, lecturer, and director of student theatrical productions. He had every reason to think that his future as a college or university professor

was secure. Young, however, believed that he had not yet realized his artistic potential and that in an academic atmosphere
he would never be able to devote the necessary time to creative
work. He had published two volumes of poetry, eight one-act
plays, and a large number of critical essays in prestigious national
magazines. Nevertheless, his decision to cut his ties with academia and strike out on his own as a free-lance writer in New
York was a measure both of his ambition and his self-confidence.

Chapter Three
Director and Drama Critic

During the two decades that separated Stark Young's graduate study at Columbia and his return to New York from Amherst, events here and abroad were moving swiftly to change radically the conditions, practices, and attitudes toward the production of plays. Perhaps most notable was the "new stagecraft" that had begun about the turn of the century with Adolphe Appia's revolution in the staging of Wagner's operas and the appearance of Gordon Craig's work on *The Art of the Theatre* (1911). In 1912 American audiences saw the results of the new approach for the first time in Max Reinhardt's production of *Sumurun*, a mime play derived from tales of the Arabian Nights. Although Stark Young was in Texas at this time, he undoubtedly knew about the performance and its significance. The period also saw the rise of the Moscow Art Theatre as a repertory theatre noted for its ensemble playing under the direction of Constantin Stanislavsky. Although they might differ in language and in applications, these men essentially held in common the premise that the performance of a play (or opera) was a synthesis of all the arts that contributed to its production—a concept that would have a place in Stark Young's drama theory—and that the actor must interpret a role in terms of his concept of the inner life of the character he was portraying. As a result of their work, scenery, lighting, and acting were coordinated to produce an integrated effect. Stanislavsky, especially, objected to artificiality, poor acting, and the glorification of the "star" at the expense of the ensemble. He developed a "system" for training actors that profoundly affected acting both in Europe and the United States.

For the most part, reforms in stagecraft, acting, and production techniques came to the American theatre not by such commercial producers as Charles Frohman and David Belasco but by small amateur groups in little theatre productions. Young's one-act plays and experiments in Texas with the Curtain Club were a part of this movement. Other better known examples would include the Irish players from Dublin's Abbey Theatre (1904); the Washington Square Players (1915) that after World War I became the Theatre Guild; the Neighborhood Playhouse (1915); the Provincetown Players (1915), reorganized in 1923 as the Experimental Players; and the Detroit Arts and Crafts Theatre (1916). Several of these organizations developed from amateur into professional or semiprofessional ensembles. In them such men as Robert Edmond Jones, Kenneth Macgowan, Eugene O'Neill, Richard Boleslavsky, Lee Simonson, Philip Moeller, Lawrence Langner, and many others hotly debated every aspect of the theatre from playwriting to the smallest detail of production. Under the leadership of these gifted men, plays originally staged by amateurs often became highly successful and ultimately reached Broadway. To this general movement and, specifically, to the Provincetown and Theatre Guild groups, Stark Young made important contributions.

The Critic

In October 1921, when Young arrived in New York, he already had connections with the *New Republic* and *Theatre Arts.* Brilliant reviews like that of Jacob Ben-Ami's performance in Sven Lange's *Samson and Delilah,* which Alexander Woollcott called the "ablest writing" in the 1920–21 season, had led Croly to make Young a contributing editor. When Francis Hackett, the regular drama critic, retired early in 1922, Young was named in his place.[1] Edith Isaacs, editor in chief of *Theatre Arts,* was also quick to recognize Young's abilities. For the past two years, she had published his work in the magazine with increasing frequency; and in January 1922 she made Young, along with Kenneth Macgowan, an associate editor. In the next few years Young was to work closely with Macgowan in productions of O'Neill's *Welded* and Molière's *George Dandin.* Young's association with both the *New Republic* and *Theatre Arts* brought him into contact with Willard and Dorothy Straight, who provided the financial backing for the founding of both periodicals. After Straight's death in 1918, Mrs. Straight married Leonard Knight Elmhirst, and they continued to support both publications. The

Elmhirsts became warm admirers of Stark Young both as a person and as a man of letters.[2]

During the 1921–22 and 1922–23 seasons, Stark Young firmly established himself as a major critic. In addition to book reviews and articles not directly relating to the New York stage, Young published forty-eight essays in the *New Republic,* twelve in *Theatre Arts,* seven in *Vanity Fair,* and five in the *North American Review.* In them he developed the major patterns that he would follow in a thousand and more subsequent articles he would write during his career. Writing for weekly and monthly periodicals, he enjoyed a distinct advantage over his newspaper colleagues. Whereas most of them felt obliged to publish their reviews on the morning or evening after opening night, Young felt no compulsion either to review every play or to review it immediately after its opening. He could attend only the performances he thought would be significant, study the text of the play, attend a second time if necessary, and write and rewrite his material. All too often, newspaper critics felt pressure (as Young did in 1924–25 when he served as critic for the *New York Times*) to make their reviews "advertisements" for the plays. Herbert Croly was a staunch supporter of the arts, and at the *New Republic* Young enjoyed a great deal of freedom, independence, and writing time.

Because of this somewhat unique position, Young's "reviews" often did not conform to the usual practice of including plot synopses, comments on acting and perhaps scenery, and hastily considered overall evaluations of play productions. Instead, Young's "reviews" may be more properly described as essays upon the art of the theatre as illustrated by a particular Broadway production. He felt no need to evaluate the production from every aspect. If a plot summary helped him to establish a point, Young included it; but, as often as not, he dispensed with it to save space for more extended analyses or discussions about such aspects of theatre art as idea, style, direction, setting, lighting, costuming, acting, and stage management. Frequently, Young began his article with a definition of a standard of performance, or a principle of art, or a distinction among terms; and in the remainder of his comments he applied the principle to the specific example or practice at hand. Anyone reading his articles over a period of time would find himself more and more involved in the principles that govern art and that make art in the theatre different from other arts. As concerned as he was with the principle or standard, Young never failed to make the direct application even when it came to naming names and citing illustrations of mistakes in acting, directing, scenery, and costuming. Almost without exception, however, when Young found fault with an individual, he made a suggestion for improvement; and although he could be caustically severe upon entire productions, he often could find in them moments or parts that he thought beautiful.

In the light of Young's academic background, his criticism is surprisingly free from academic coloring. Dogmatic in the best sense, it derives from principles of art that to Young were clearly defined. Criticism of specific performances of plays in the theatre is often ephemeral, since the commentary relates almost wholly to a given effect on a given evening that cannot be precisely re-created. What saves Young's work from ephemerality is his constant reference to a standard or principle from which his judgment is made. To read Young's essays is to take a course in art, specifically, the art of the theatre, which Young considered different from all other arts. At times, however, one does encounter in his writing a certain vagueness that renders his meaning difficult to establish. Often, one cannot be certain that someone else, armed with Young's standards or principles, would make the same judgment in a given instance that Young makes. The answer lies partly in the fact that into Young's judgments go not only the principles of art but also all of Young's learning and his personal sensitivity or taste. Young himself would probably have admitted the role of the individual's sensitivity and taste in critical judgments.

About some of the "modern" movements in the theatre, Stark Young held well defined attitudes. Although he respected the theory of realism, which he defined as a reliance "strictly on external details to express whatever meaning is desired," he thought the method had not produced many good plays.[3] In Russia, he conceded, realism had resulted in "truthfulness, simplicity, and a lack of marked form," and in Ibsen it had also voiced an authentic note. But in America it had produced mainly problem and sociological plays, none of which "took any great strides or went very far." (To this general rule, Young felt the first acts of Eugene O'Neill's *Diff'rent* and *Anna Christie* were exceptions.) In reviewing John Howard Lawson's *Roger Bloomer* and Elmer L. Rice's *The Adding Machine,* Young defined expressionism as a theatrical method "by which any means whatever . . . may be used to reveal the content of a dramatic moment . . . to give us the very soul of the incident."⁴ Neither play, decided Young, was successful. In *Roger Bloomer,* he could find no unity of idea; and in *The Adding Machine* Young noted that Rice had written a play "not so much about life as about expressionism" and had used the method not to reveal but to entertain. In dealing with both realism and expressionism, Young was more concerned to examine the two methods in terms of their potential for great drama than to dissect the plays at hand.

Early in 1923 Young with thousands of other New Yorkers welcomed the first visit of the Moscow Art Theatre to this country. In large measure it represented the kind of permanent company of directors, actors, and supporting personnel that such groups as the Provincetown Players and later the Group Theatre wished to see established in this country. For years the Russians had been presenting the same plays they performed here, and most New York critics, who were somewhat disadvantaged because the actors spoke only in Russian, praised, even overpraised, their performances. The company presented five major plays. Young saw them all but confined his remarks about them to a single essay. He thought Tolstoy's *Isar Fyodor Ivanovitch* very disappointing. Although he recognized fine acting, superb costumes, and authentic settings in the staging, he remained "quite unmoved, indifferent" because the production was not unified by the projection of "the idea" of the sixteenth century.⁵ The company had not translated historical realities (which Young observed he could find in museums) into ideas and stage terms that would make them art. In Maxim Gorky's *The Lower Depths,* he also observed passages of excellent acting, but "what let me down and left me dashed and disappointed was the broken quality of the performance as a whole." Character after character, wrote Young, "stood out to the eye, heavily accented, without a blur." The players did not function smoothly as an ensemble, and the production separated into parts. But the performances of Chekhov's *The Cherry Orchard* and *The Three Sisters* were almost flawless. In them Young found every element of the production supporting and illuminating one idea. Declared Young, "I saw Chekhov's art come true," and added that he now understood the likeness of Chekhov's method to that of Shakespeare. Young summed up the meaning of the Moscow Art Theatre to the American theatre by saying that the Russians represented a group of sincere artists who have been "working together thoroughly and through many years, in an organization, and under a distinguished and sympathetic leader, and for a devoted public."[6] In making this judgment, Young voiced the aspirations of many persons dedicated to the theatre for just such an organization in America.

Among the Moscow performers, Young admired the work of Richard Boleslavsky, Maria Ouspenskya, and Stanislavsky, himself, though he believed Stanislavsky's acting in the role of Satine in Gorky's *The Lower Depths* had "long since become academic" and "a recollection of a thing once created."[7] But despite the fame of the Russian company, Young knew there were actors just as good, even better, outside of Russia. In his judgment Sarah Bernhardt was the greatest actress he ever saw,[8] but throughout his career he considered Eleonora Duse the greatest artist in the theatre because she embodied "the fundamentals of all art." Even in her old age, Duse in Gallerati-Scotti's *Così Sia* (*So Be It*) illustrated "first of all the principle in art of the necessity of the artist's own greatness, his sensitivity and power in feeling, in idea, in soul, in the education and fine culture of all these."[9] She represented Young's highest standard in acting. In her, form became identical with idea. He cited Doris Keane, whose performance in Edward Sheldon's *Romance* several years earlier Young had praised as an example of natural "talent." After seeing her in *The Czarina*, Young remarked that only her talent made it worthwhile to review the play; but despite her talent, she did not have a consistent idea of what kind of person Catherine was or might have been.[10]

Among actors Young praised the work of Giovanni Grasso, Jacob Ben-Ami, and John Barrymore. On occasion, Grasso's work could become "inevitable, searching, unpredictable, necessary, inspired."[11] About Ben-Ami, with whom Young had formed a strong friendship, the critic emphasized the actor's deep sincerity and "profound desire for all the most varied

and passionate and beautiful forms of dramatic writing; and a
taste and long training for the needed repertory system."[12] In
reviewing John Barrymore's Hamlet, Young called it the most
satisfying he had seen, while pointing out the actor's occasional
lapses in the reading of the verse and his inability to render
"decreasing emotion."[13]

Young's straightforward appraisal of both the strengths and
weaknesses of performers gained for him their respect, at times
their fear, and in many instances their friendship. Likewise, his
enthusiastic endorsement of Robert Edmond Jones's genius for
stage settings and his early appreciation of Eugene O'Neill as
a playwright endeared him to those who sought to advance
the "new theatre" movement.[14] Accepting him as one of them,
the Theatre Guild in the fall of 1923 invited him to direct
their production of René Lenormand's The Failures.

The Director

Les Ratés, by the French modernist, performed first during
World War I in Geneva and subsequently in various European
cities, was hardly a play to attract large audiences. Translated
as The Failures, it recounted in fourteen scenes the grim, unhappy
story of two young lovers known only as "He" and "She."
"He" is a bad poet who wants to become a playwright, and
"She" is a poor actress. Essentially they fail because their ambitions exceed their abilities. As scene follows scene, they descend
lower into the depths of failure, sustained only by their love
for each other, until at last he strangles her and shoots himself.
The play, as Young remarked, turns upon the degradation, confusion, and dirt in men's lives ennobled only at times by the
purity of love that moves within them.[15]

The Failures opened at the Garrick Theater on 19 November
1923 and ran for forty performances. In directing it, Young
sought to find the central idea in each of the scenes and to
simplify the movement within them. "I tried especially to keep
them," said Young, "from being cluttered with movement and
action and a foolish attempt to imitate the details of life."[16]
The settings, designed by Lee Simonson, supported Young's
desire for unity of movement. A slender Gothic pillar, for example, with light filtering through invisible stained glass, sufficed

to suggest a cathedral. In directing the play, Young first discussed with each actor the meaning of the character he would play, permitted the actor to interpret the role as he saw it, and then selected the best and most promising features in his work for further development. Young wanted the role to be expressed as far as possible in the actor's own terms. The director's object was to "get as much truth as possible in the material out of which the actor's performance is built; the actor's problem consists in his getting the mental rhythm of the lines, the exact emotional stress that will go into the words."[17]

The Failures was an artistic success. Writing in the *North American Review,* Young called the production "an important and courageous experiment on the part of the Guild." He remarked that Jacob Ben-Ami in the role of the poet acted "with great pathos and magnificent power in the deeper scenes," while the "settings and direction achieved the full quality of the Lenormand method."[18] Young's judgment was fully supported by the critics. In the *Nation,* Ludwig Lewisohn praised Young's direction and the acting of Ben-Ami and Winifred Lenihan as the lovers. The reviewer for the *Boston Evening Transcript* noted that Young kept "to the pervading, the essential, humanity" of the play; "he is truthful without dryness on the one hand or over-emphasis on the other. He knits details into the expanding web, and they have meaning. In the definition of character he is exact but not rigid. . . . Mr. Young as producer is never visible, but always present. The players ably second him."[19] Thornton Wilder, in a letter to Young, declared that the production would haunt him as long as he lived and described it as "so beautiful, so beautiful."[20] The consensus of contemporary critics was that *The Failures* was one of the finest plays ever produced by the Guild Theatre, though it was not a popular success, possibly because, as Lawrence Langner suggested, the title discouraged the New York playgoers.[21]

Although *The Failures* did not enjoy tremendous success at the box-office, Young's direction was warmly endorsed by the critics and by his associates in the Guild. The play had scarcely been withdrawn before Young was rehearsing Eugene O'Neill's *Welded,* whose melancholy plot of marital bickering was somewhat similar to that of *The Failures.* In *Welded,* a young playwright and an actress, who have been married five years, learn through incessant quarreling that they cannot live without each other, although the bond that holds them together is hate. Jacob Ben-Ami again played the leading role of the male lover, while for the actress wife Young chose Doris Keane. Then at the height of her powers, Doris Keane had had an astonishing career. After her debut in 1903 in Henry Arthur Jones's *Whitewashing Julia,* she played in a number of successful Broadway productions. In 1913 she became a sensation in the lead role of Edward Sheldon's *Romance.* Two years later, she took the play to London, where she appeared in it 1,049 times before the run ended in 1918. Afterwards, Young had admired her talent in the title role of *The Czarina* by Melchoir Lengyel and Lajos Biro. With her Young shared a personal relationship that may have come close to marriage and lasted until her death in 1945.[22] Unfortunately, her part in *Welded* was not particularly well suited to her style of acting.

Welded, produced at the Thirty-Ninth Street Theatre by Kenneth Macgowan, Robert Edmond Jones, and Eugene O'Neill, opened on 17 March 1924 and ran for twenty-four performances. The production was recognized as "easily one of the most important events of the theatrical season,"[23] yet critics called it gloomy, monotonous, uninspiring, in fact, dull. Only the settings of Robert Edmond Jones and the acting of Ben-Ami and Doris Keane under Young's direction saved it from being a flat failure. The general reaction of the reviewers was that "Mr. Young, as director, and Mr. Jones, as creator of the settings, have done all things possible to persuade the handling of emphasis and beauty. But they are dealing with very heavy timber."[24] Young himself characterized *Welded* as having only "a fair success." For his part, remarked Young, "the end I sought . . . was to make the directing of the play on the stage inseparable from the meaning, in every way, of the whole thing."[25] In view of the content of the play, Young's success in realizing it on the stage may have contributed to its lack of audience appeal.

The day after *Welded* closed, on 5 April, Macgowan, Jones, and O'Neill produced Molière's *George Dandin,* translated and directed by Stark Young, at the Provincetown Playhouse, as a curtain raiser to a dramatization of Coleridge's "The Ancient Mariner," arranged by O'Neill. In directing the Molière comedy about a cuckolded husband baffled by his own flirtatious wife, Young said his intention was "to put on the whole a hint of extra style—style in the sense of an added luster and vivacity, a dash of artifice and elaboration." He saw the play primarily as "an artificial piece of art."[26] Although his handling of the classic comedy was admired by many, John Corbin, critic for the *New York Times,* complained that Young achieved a "facile laughter" through an artificial treatment of the piece. Conceding that the audience "gave evidence of sustained interest and at the close applauded loudly," Corbin felt that Young had missed much of Molière's intent.[27] The comment suggests that the director achieved his intention but that the critic held a different concept of the play. For a program of this nature, the two pieces, performed thirty-three times, may be said to have enjoyed a moderate success.

The Saint

The summer of 1923 Stark Young spent in Italy writing three plays—*The Colonnade, The Saint,* and *Rose Windows*—first at Assisi and later at Palermo, where he thought he worked best. By the time he returned to New York to begin rehearsals for *The Failures,* he had completed *The Saint,* probably *The Colon nade,* and, possibly, *Rose Windows. The Saint* (and, perhaps, *The Colonnade*) he wrote specifically for Ben-Ami, who, after reading it, expressed his eagerness to perform the role. During November and December, the directors of the Guild considered the play, and in their discussions Young urged them to think only in terms of Ben-Ami for the part. Young wrote to Philip Moeller, one of the Guild directors, that *The Saint* was "obviously written in terms of Ben-Ami and . . . if he were not in it much would be written in words that is not there now—obviously." While rehearsing it, Young said, he and the actor would "add what is necessary. It is libretto to his quality."[28] By early May 1924, when Young left to spend another summer in Italy, the Guild had scheduled *The Saint* for fall production. Happy at this prospect, Young wrote a friend that "it will be wonderfully acted at least."[29] At Portofino, Young polished the lines of *The Saint* and looked forward to the fall when he expected both *The Saint* and *The Colonnade* to be performed. In August, *Theatre Arts* published *The Colonnade,* and Young accepted the position of theatre critic for the *New York Times.* On 11 October, Young's forty-third birthday, *The Saint* opened at the Greenwich Village Theatre.

Young's play begins on the portico of a seminary in Las Flores, a town on the border between the Southwest and Mexico; the time is Good Friday. At the rear of the stage is a statue of the Virgin Mother, Mary of the Seven Times Wounded Heart. Kneeling before her is a young man named Valdez. He has endured a lonely boyhood on a ranch, spending much of his time dreaming or "talking about time and going on, and life never going back." Now he is a student in the seminary, and in two years he can be expected to become a priest. But his priestly ambition is opposed by his love for Marietta, a wild young girl who has run off with the acting company of Tip Thompson. Now that she has returned for a brief stay, she admits to her uncle Pacho that there is something in Valdez that she cannot get out of her mind. After Marietta and Valdez meet and pledge their love for each other, the religious procession that is to take the statue to the cathedral passes across the stage. The procession and the music that accompanies it suggest the basic theme of the play, defined by Young as "continuity, going on, the long line of the soul's days that makes life possible to bear."[30]

In act 2, the scene shifts to Aguas Calientes, where Valdez, who has left the seminary, and Marietta are appearing in Tip Thompson's Variety Show. Among the variety acts are those of American Pigeons (in the original play bill she is called Paris Pigeons), who performs with trained pigeons; Dedaux, the French Creole knife thrower; and the pantomime of the comic Old Doctor and the Three Beautiful Daughters. As the final act, Valdez performs an imitation of Charlie Chaplin. While most of the acts have not been very well received, that of Valdez has become the hit of the show. As the players rehearse their routines, the audience learns from Tip Thompson and Pigeons that Dedaux has taken Marietta away from Valdez.

Act 3 takes place mainly in the rehearsal room and belongs primarily to Marietta and Dedaux. Beyond the rehearsal room is the stage, and one can hear the audience occasionally applaud as the variety show continues. While Valdez is performing, Mar-

ietta and Dedaux agree to leave the show together. Tired of
Valdez's sad eyes and his long face, Marietta has turned to Dedaux, whom she both hates and loves passionately. After they
have departed, Valdez receives an ovation from the audience
and comes back to the rehearsal room. Pigeons, who can scarcely
conceal her love for Valdez, gives him a pistol and tells him
that Marietta has run away with Dedaux. But Valdez refuses
to pursue them and stands on the stage by himself, a lonely
figure doing nothing.

The final act takes place back at the seminary a year after
the opening scene of act 1. Again it is Good Friday, and the
processional music is heard afar off. Valdez has left the Tip
Thompson show. He feels that he is not a born artist. "I'm
not miserable," he says, "if I don't put myself into something,
as an artist must be. I've got no hunger to pour myself out.
What I want is to flow into myself. . . . To go on forever in
my own truth." Of one matter he is certain: "in life we can
never go back, there's no going back." He does not see his
way clearly to the future, but he knows that he will see "the
long line of the soul's days that makes life possible to bear."[31]
He must "go on." As the sounds of the procession are heard,
Marietta and Dedaux approach from a side street. She cannot
forget Valdez. Dedaux has become indifferent to her. As Valdez
encounters them, Marietta thinks he is going to use his pistol;
but Valdez realizes that she is not worth his love and lets them
go. The procession passes, but Valdez does not drop to his
knees before the Virgin as he did a year ago. In the stage directions to the published play, Young interprets Valdez's feelings:
as the statue of Christ follows that of the Virgin, Valdez's loneli-
ness pours out, and the tragedy of Christ overwhelms him. Valdez kneels before the statue, then rises, takes a few steps
suggesting his Charlie Chaplin routine, hesitates, and moves
toward the seminary door. But as he approaches it, he says
"No!" He walks out of the portico and disappears along the
street. His life must go on, and he cannot turn back either to
the seminary or to an artistic career.

The Saint had many elements of a very successful play and
was beautifully staged. The two basic sets—the seminary and
the rehearsal room of the variety show, and the procession (including the lighted statues of the Virgin and Christ)—designed

by Robert Edmond Jones, were thought by audiences to be strikingly beautiful. Macklin Marrow's music, performed by musicians in the procession, provided a powerful, discordant, and weird backdrop for the action. The costumes of the seminary students, the marchers in the procession, and the actors in the variety troop were notable for brilliant color and artistic design.

The entire production, moreover, had a distinct Mexican and Italian atmosphere. The portico of the seminary reminded playgoers of both Mexico and Italy. Even more reminiscent of Italy, however, was the village procession which Alexander Woollcott thought "the finest and most stirring thing in this play." It was, as he wrote, "brilliantly reproduced on the Greenwich Village stage—a shuffling, colorful procession, astir with the dust and the memories of ancient pieties."[32] He would remember it always. In describing it, Woollcott quoted Young's lengthy account of a village procession he had witnessed in Italy and recorded in *The Three Fountains*. Equally impressive were the Old Doctor and the Three Beautiful Daughters, whose immediate source was an extemporized act in a variety show called "The Three Suitors of Seville" seen a few years earlier by Robert Edmond Jones in New Mexico. Both this pantomime and that of Valdez had their origin in the Italian and French Commedia dell'Arte of the sixteenth century.

Young's play enjoyed a moderate success, but it should have done much better than it did. The problem lay in the acting. In writing it, Young depended almost entirely upon the acting of Ben-Ami to carry the subtleties of the theme; but for some unexplained reason, Ben-Ami did not act the role. Instead, the part was given to Leo Carrillo, whose acting Woollcott described as "inert and groggy." Instead of conveying the nuances of Valdez's complex character, Carrillo seems only to have made Valdez a stupid young man. Most of the supporting actors were equally flat and dull. The only outstanding performance in the entire production was that of Maria Ouspenskaya, recently of the Moscow Art Theater, who, as Pigeons, was playing her first role in English. Young admired her work extravagantly and throughout their long friendship addressed her as "Pigeons." In defense of the actors, however, one should remark that the play presented formidable challenges even to the best of performers.

Shortly after *The Saint* closed, Stark Young wrote Sherwood Anderson that it was "amateurishly cast, and so lost its effect and naturally . . . my fellow critics went for it."[33] Reviewers generally blamed the acting while admiring the play itself. Woollcott wondered what it would have been like had it been at all well played. Others found it a play written with "great delicacy and possessing many moments of beauty," a fine piece of writing not vitalized by its performance. Carrillo was seen as earnest but not magnetic, "a steady but uninspired worker in a role that calls for a flaming performance if all the values of the story are to emerge."[34] The consensus of the hostile critics was that the play was too intellectual and artistic for the taste of the usual Broadway theatergoer. Percy Hammond and George Jean Nathan uttered the harshest complaints. While conceding that his opinions were not those of a "high hatter," Hammond characterized the play as "a dull, shambling, inarticulate bit of wistful playwriting, full of endeavor and empty of effect."[35] Attacking Young personally, Nathan wrote that "the character of Valdez . . . serves at once as an unwitting metaphysical autobiography of the author and as a criticism of him. The inarticulateness, the befuddlement and the obscurity of the character, groping boozily [Valdez does not drink in the play] and uncertainly for truth and beauty, are the inarticulateness, the befuddlement and the obscurity of Young." Later in his review, however, Nathan voiced his basic animus when he wrote that " 'The Saint' is a fairly good play, but it is not a good enough play for one who criticizes other plays as Young criticizes them."[36]

The Colonnade

In light of the general agreement of those who saw *The Saint* that its fatal defect was the inability of the cast to project its meaning convincingly, Young's withdrawal of *The Colonnade* from consideration by the Provincetown Players is understandable. Without the right cast, this play, which is almost wholly dependent upon its Southern setting and Southern traditions, would doubtless have little chance for success in New York. Young was probably correct when he wrote that he felt that it would have been "slaughtered by the actors available."[37] One

would like to know what he would have thought of the performance of *The Colonnade* by the London Stage Society in April
1925, starring Reginald Dance and Henry Oscar.[38] This production, which Young did not see, received favorable reviews. The
critic for the *Manchester Guardian* thought it applied Chekhov's
idiom to the humdrum family life of the Southern states and
compared its "Flora House" to the landscape of *The Cherry
Orchard.*[39] Arthur Bingham Walkley, drama critic for the *Times*
(London), after calling the play "a work of art of absorbing
interest," remarked that "it is as near the 'static' theatre of
Maeterlinck as anything we can think of. It has the Maeterlinckian vagueness, and the Maeterlinckian melancholy, and the
Maeterlinckian benignity to poor human nature."[40] In view of
Young's subsequent use of *The Colonnade* as the basis of a novel,
Walkley's concluding suggestion that the play might have been
"infinitely more suitable to the methods of the novel" seems
almost a prophecy.

The Colonnade, set in Mississippi (Young was probably thinking of Como), deals with a dispute over the inheritance of land.
Two brothers, Alexander and Ned Dandridge, could have expected to inherit their father's estate of about two thousand
acres. As a young man, however, Ned alienated his father by
living a wild life, gambling, drinking, and ruinous borrowing
from disreputable characters. As a consequence, Ned was disinherited, and the several hundred acres of rich land that should
have gone to him went to his brother, Alexander. Years later,
Ned died; and as the play begins, Ned, his son, brings suit to
recover the land that his father did not inherit.

The Dandridge family has always lived at Flower House. A
Southern mansion built before the Civil War, its most unusual
architectural feature is a colonnade in the garden. Amid the
old roses and jasmine that are in bloom, it is a place of beauty
for young John Dandridge; but it also seems to represent a
"particular streak" (523) in the family. His mother loved it;
yet his father, Major Dandridge, has cared nothing about it
and except for his son would have pulled it down. For John,
the colonnade symbolizes his love for the South: "I always
know," he says, "when it's like this that I love my own country
best after all, my own South" (543).

Besides Major Dandridge, a fine looking man, age seventy,

whose appearance suggests General Robert E. Lee, John's two aunts, Ellen and May, reside permanently at Flower House. Mr. Bobo, a plump, hearty gentleman of sixty, has been visiting the family for the past month and expects to remain several months longer. Cousin Tom, an elderly man with an elegant appearance, presently studying the realization of biblical prophecies in Southern history, has been visiting at Flower House for the past three years and shows no sign of leaving. The Major would not think of asking them to leave, because they are gentlemen and old friends as well.

When John, now age twenty-four, was three years old, his mother left her husband. John has grown up in the care of his father and his aunts. Ambitious to become a writer, John has spent the past year in New York and Europe and very recently returned to Flower House. He has scarcely been home for ten days when his father sends him to Kentucky to see his dying mother. John meets her for the first time since he was a baby and realizes that he has grown up misjudging her. Far from the "bad" woman he had always thought her, she is beautiful and good. On the way back to Flower House from her funeral, John marries Evelyn Oliver in Memphis and reaches home just as a lawyer affirms to Major Dandridge that "Cousin Ned" has no claim upon the land.

Major Dandridge, who has always kept any knowledge of this land dispute from his son, can no longer delay an explanation of the matter. Although the Major insists upon the legality of his claim to the entire estate, John argues that "there's no reason why this man [Cousin Ned] should pay so for his father's being wild." The legal aspect is not the issue. To take the land from Cousin Ned is "the kind of thing we just don't do, that's all" (538). If his father will not give Cousin Ned the land, John will go to New York, earn money from his writing, and endeavor to pay Cousin Ned the value of the land. To persuade his son to agree with him, the Major enlists the support of John's bride. She is to use his sexual passion for her to gain his acquiescence. In a moment of weakness, John agrees, but the next morning he tells her he cannot keep his promise.

As the gap between the father and son widens, the dispute takes on another dimension. When John was a baby, Ned returned to see his father (John's grandfather). At Mrs. Dan-

dridge's suggestion, the Major invited Ned to stay for a visit.
Ned accepted and remained much longer than the Major expected. Ned and Mrs. Dandridge became very close; and one
night after the Major had seen them walking in the colonnade,
she asked her husband to return the land to Ned. The Major
thought she was in love with Ned. She denied any wrongdoing.
She left home but said she would return when the Major wanted
her. He never gave in; she never came back.

Thus, John has taken the same position that his mother took,
and in so doing he implicitly condemns his father's actions.
John realizes that his father is actually still fighting his mother.
He exclaims: "It's not money, not family, not principles! Oh,
no! It's this damned feeling against my mother!" (555). John
begins to understand that his father—and perhaps his grandfather—has placed holding the land or estate intact above human
values and by refusing to change his position has allowed the
beauty and affection of his wife to escape him. The Major with
all his politeness, polish, and affection for his son is but a striking
illustration of the trouble that afflicts everyone at Flower House,
perhaps of the South itself.

Suddenly John wonders if he can stand it: "the place, the
days and nights passing . . . and all this gentleness and fineness
and this affection and good breeding. . . . so much understanding and such endless patience, no matter how far off the question
is! . . . you are at the mercy of life in this place." He finds it
all the more terrible "because it *is* so beautiful." As he contemplates the old people—his father, his aunts, Cousin Tom, and
Mr. Bobo—he knows that each is right in his own way. "And
all of them gradually getting older and going to pieces! And
loving me and wanting me to have my own life! And everyone
keeping up his standard of living, trying to converse whether
he feels like it or not, everyone holding himself to the idea
he has of how things ought to be" (551). Like Quentin Compson
years later in *Absalom, Absalom!,* John will protest that he does
not hate them or the South. But they are standing still, and
John knows—as Valdez did in *The Saint*—that "life in us can
never go back or stay fixed, but must always go on" (529).
From this protective covering, John wants to be free, not only
from the old people but also from his wife. If he is to become
a writer or an artist, he must be free, "without any obstruction
to whatever works in me, whatever reflection of life, whatever

flies off from things" (553). Without pausing to say goodbye, John takes the train north.

Underlying both *The Saint* and *The Colonnade* were intensely personal implications for Stark Young. The Italian coloring of the religious procession in *The Saint* and its setting along the border between the Southwest and Mexico reflected Young's own fondness for Italy and his trips into Mexico from Texas. Even more personal was its theme, embodied in Valdez, that the individual must press on through his experiences in life without turning back, since Young saw that he had gone from a boyhood in Como to a teaching career in Mississippi, Texas, and Massachusetts to the theatre world of New York. Now a writer and critic, he could never go back.

The Colonnade was even more personal to Young, since in it Young looked back squarely upon the life he had known in Mississippi and his liberation from it. In *The Colonnade,* moreover, he voiced for the first time his mixed feelings toward the South. Like John Dandridge, Young loved the people of the South; they were his own people, "my own South." He loved his two maiden aunts, who could have been, and very likely were, the prototypes of the two aunts in the Dandridge family. The essentially good but tiresome "guests" who came to visit but remained as family dependents Young had known in his own and other Southern families (and would write about again). Perhaps the most personal of all aspects of the play, however, was Young's relationship to his father and mother. Toward her, Young cherished a tender and loving memory that would admit no criticism. Young loved and respected his father, but at times he felt keenly his father's underlying opposition to his son's artistic impulses. Toward them all, Young recognized his ambivalent feelings. Loyally he loved them, even when they were tiresome, and he loved the South with which he identified them; but he knew also that he could not live his life in the South. The place was "sick with the unexpressed." Like the South itself, they were constantly covering reality with a self-deceiving veneer. Young felt that he could never go back to this kind of life. Without ever joining the Vanderbilt Fugitives (and later the Agrarians), Young had already become a fugitive and anticipated in life and in his writings a number of their central ideas.

CARNEGIE LIBRARY
LIVINGSTONE COLLEGE
SALISBURY, N. C. 28144

Chapter Four

Theatre Criticism

By 1923, when Stark Young published *The Flower in Drama,* his first book on drama theory, his reviews in the *New Republic,* his activities as director, and his own playwriting had established him as an authority on the drama and a spokesman for the new developments in the American theatre. From his platforms on *Theatre Arts* and the *New Republic,* he lectured actors, directors, producers, and playwrights alike; and such men as Kenneth Macgowan, Eugene O'Neill, Robert Edmond Jones, and Richard Boleslavsky listened respectfully to Young's opinions. His creativity during the early and middle years of the 1920s is astonishing. In addition to the plays he wrote and directed and the weekly essays he contributed to the *New Republic,* between 1923 and 1927 Young published four books on the theatre— *The Flower in Drama* (1923), *Glamour* (1925), *Theatre Practice* (1926), and *The Theater* (1927)—and two books of essays— *The Three Fountains* (1924) and *Encaustics* (1926). In these volumes he embodied his concepts of art and theatre, as well as the basic principles from which his drama criticism evolved. For four of these, and for most of his later work, he had the immense advantage of Maxwell Perkins's superb editing and literary counsel, as well as the prestige of the Scribner's publishing firm.

The Flower in Drama

Primarily, Stark Young's *The Flower in Drama* is a treatise upon acting as one of the several arts that comprise the theatre.[1] For fourteen of its fifteen chapters, Young used with some revisions and additions essays that he had published in the *New Republic* and *Theatre Arts* during 1921 and 1922. The fifteenth chapter, "Letter to Duse," had not been previously published. The volume begins with an essay on acting—the longest and most important chapter in the book—that sets the substantive limits for the remainder of the work. Young devotes succeeding chapters to identifying the essential qualities of acting as illustrated in the performance of such actors as Jacob Ben-Ami, Charlie Chaplin, Ruth Draper, Doris Keane, Giovanni Grasso, and Eleonora Duse. In other chapters he considers a variety of special topics: acting in the nineteenth century, the movies and the Italian circus, the Jewish and Yiddish theatre in New York, the handling of poetry in acting, and the human voice as a crucial element in acting. Near the end of the work, Young devotes two chapters, "The Flower" and "Translations," to a discussion of the distinction between art and reality. When put beside the initial chapter on "Acting," these essays place his theory of acting in the larger perspective of his concept of art and become the basis of much of his subsequent writing.

For Young, art consists of that which the artist adds to nature (reality). "Nature was never art," wrote Young in the earlier essay from which the chapter on "Acting" was taken.[2] Art, in whatever form it takes, translates life or actuality into its own terms and adds something that was not there before. If an artist were to reach a point where his work duplicates or becomes reality, his work would no longer be art. To be art, something must be added, that is, art must always differ from reality. (This premise accounts for much of Young's objection to the realistic movement in the theatre.)

In the chapter on "The Flower" (originally published as a review of the *Nō Plays of Japan* translated by Arthur Whaley),[3] Young offers an example of the difference between art and reality. He observes that the fourteenth-century Seami, the head of the Nō, taught that in imitation there must always be something of the unlike, because if one presses imitation too far, it will "impinge on reality and will cease to give an impression of likeness. If one aims at only the beautiful, the flower . . . will be sure to appear" (138). To illustrate, Young writes that if the actor taking the role of an old man merely imitates the characteristics of old age (bent back, crooked knees, shrunken frame, etc.), the "flower" will be lacking; there will be no beauty in the impersonation. Instead, the actor should study to portray an old man's will or desire to talk correctly without having the ability. This effect could be achieved by the actor making his movements a little late. The example also illustrates Young's belief that acting is not merely imitation or mimicry but an art. The actor represents but does not reproduce.

Applying this concept to the theatre, Young insists that the art of the theatre is not merely a combination of such matters as setting, actors, music, direction, and costume; rather, the art of the theatre is a "distinct and separate art" (150), and none of these components remains the same when translated into terms of the theatre. In the chapter on "Translations," Young uses Robert Edmond Jones's setting for *The Birthday of the Infanta* to illustrate his point. The buildings in Jones's setting could never be found in Spain; but one could find in Spain the "barbaric and cruel barrenness" (151) and cold elegance that characterize Jones's architecture. In other words, Jones has not reproduced Spanish architecture but has accomplished a translation or restatement of architecture into theatre terms. Likewise, the costumes in this pantomime are not copies of actual Spanish seventeenth-century clothes but rather those clothes seen in terms of the theatre. Young concludes that in theatre arts, as in all other arts, "the reality must be restated in terms of the art concerned before there is any art at all. . . . An element must be there which was not there before. . . . It must be the same and not the same, like the moon in water, by a certain nameless difference born anew" (154). At the conclusion of the chapter on "Acting," Young states the same concept in slightly different terms: "This is the object of all art, to create in reality abstraction and in abstraction reality; to complete, in sum, our living for us. It is this that gives to art something of the quality of a dream, the fear for its possibility, the urgency of its desire. And it is this in art that makes life follow it" (39).

Once the playwright has conceived and written the play, the most important single element in its production is the acting. To the "average" theatregoer, what makes the play real to him is the presence of actual men and women on the stage. Yet the average theatregoer is no more qualified to judge the quality of acting he sees and hears than he would be to judge the performance of a piece of music. To make judgments about the art of the theatre, one must have attended it repeatedly, viewed good and bad acting intelligently, made comparisons, and formed in his mind concepts or ideals, that is, standards by which to judge. Few members of a theatre audience possess these qualifications.

Young also dismisses those—and here he includes many actors themselves—who believe that the function of the actor is to reproduce reality. They remind him of the person who views a painting of corn and praises it because he cannot distinguish between the painted corn and the real corn, or the theatregoer who does not wish to see the actor who "died" on stage return for curtain calls. If perfect illusion is the goal of acting, a dog on stage would attain perfection, since he will always be a dog and nothing else. Such notions are wrongheaded, argues Young, because the object of the actor is not a reproduction of a character but a representation of it; the business of acting is the translation of its matter into another kind of truth; "acting is not art until it ceases to be life" (11).

To those who insist that the actor *becomes* the character he portrays, Young replies that the actor always remains himself, and he must be conscious of translating the thing to be created into terms of himself. The quality of acting, therefore, has a relation to the personal distinction or quality of the actor himself. As examples, Young cites Duse, Bernhardt, Chaliapin, Grasso, Nijinsky, and Chaplin, great actors, who are always themselves and never lose their identities. Much of their greatness in acting results from "the extent to which the elements of life may be gathered up in him for the spring toward luminous revelation, toward more abundant life" (14–15). For Young, the supreme example of this concept of acting was Eleonora Duse; she, more than anyone else, had the personal distinction and the inner life that gave form and substance to her art.

In addition to personal sincerity and integrity, Young insists that the actor have not only technical equipment and feeling but also an *idea,* "some Homeric phantom," with which he can identify. The actor should never play from nature direct but "from some idea—set up out of nature, if you like—in his mind." The actor, asserts Young, "plays from some imaginary being who is not his own self nor yet any self in nature" (18). Through this idea, the actor may station his role at the right distance from himself and "in the right relation to himself to make it art" (19). Actors who are great artists as well need

not confine themselves to one kind of role and need not be
tied to certain types of parts simply by their physical characteristics.

In America Young has found no actor whose art fulfills his
requirements for greatness. He has occasionally seen beautiful
acting, but no actor whose art is "complete or transcendent"
(26). Perhaps the best American actors can do is illustrated
by George M. Cohan (in the *Theatre Arts* article the example
is Al Jolson), who has talent and an understanding of technique.
But his field is a thin region, touching only the surface of American popular culture and not interpreting the depths of the American experience. The rest of American acting, according to
Young, lacks technique, good diction, gesture, and cultivation
in both actors and audiences. In a later chapter entitled "Circus,"
Young complains that the filming techniques of the movies (in
1923) are aimed solely at making money and that the constant
"takes" and "retakes" of scenes without regard to sequence
in the script would prevent even an excellent actor from achieving artistic competence.

Finally, asserts Young, acting comes back to the "presence"
of the actor, the union of his body with his mind. Neither his
voice nor his brain by itself can make good acting; what is
required is the oneness of the words and the body, through
which the actor's idea becomes manifest. "The highest use of
the body, of gesture, is not to reproduce, but to represent,
with an added radiance, what is within, not, that is, to be an
image but a symbol" (34).

Like other leaders of the new movement in the theatre, Stark
Young placed emphasis upon the improvement of acting, though
he saw it as only one of the components that contribute to
the art of the theatre. In discussing several recently published
volumes on the theatre, Montrose J. Moses remarked in the
Outlook upon Young's "calmness of judgment, which suggests
to me that he has come to the theater as critic after his aesthetic
philosophy has been shaken and enriched by the theories of
design and form and color introduced into the realm of modern
painting by Cézanne, Matisse, and others. In other words, he
[Young] gives us creative criticism, and . . . meeting with such
lucid understanding of what art comprises makes us welcome
Young in the theatre as one of the few who will help the new
movement immeasurably."[4]

Moses placed Young in the perspective of the new American movement in the creative arts which he felt had been heralded by such works as Amy Lowell's *Tendencies in Modern American Poetry* (1917), Louis Untermeyer's *The New Era in American Poetry* (1919), and John Livingston Lowes's *Convention and Revolt in Poetry* (1922). Moses noted that the "dawn of creative flowering is always preceded by statement[s] of art principles and close questioning of art technic."[5] In comparing Young's book to Kenneth Macgowan and Robert Edmond Jones's *Continental Stagecraft* (1922) and Macgowan's earlier *The Theater of Tomorrow* (1921), Moses felt that Young displayed a depth of critical perception that Macgowan lacked. Macgowan remained a disciple of the movement, whereas Young moved in the vanguard of those formulating its principles and standards.

When Charles Scribner assigned Maxwell Perkins as the firm's editor for Young's *The Flower in Drama,* the publisher initiated a warm friendship between the two men that lasted until Perkins's death in 1947. Perkins, the greatest editorial genius of the century, brought to Young's books the same rare combination of literary appreciation and meticulous care that characterized his relations with Thomas Wolfe, Ernest Hemingway, F. Scott Fitzgerald, and many others. Although more at home in fiction than in drama, Perkins recognized Young's uniqueness as a drama critic and the prestige he brought to the firm even when his books were not outstanding financial successes.

After *The Flower in Drama,* Perkins accepted Young's *The Three Fountains* (1924), a volume of sketches, studies, and essays based upon material that had appeared in the *New Republic* and the *North American Review,* but ultimately deriving from his travels in Spain and Italy.[6] Although in the totality of Young's work *The Three Fountains* is a minor achievement, it represented a departure from his drama criticism in both subject matter and treatment. In seeking to interpret Latin culture, Young was moving toward a larger audience, and the fictional episodes presaged his later successes in the novel. The book was widely reviewed, and almost without exception reviewers praised the beauty of his style and his grasp of Italian life. The reviewer for the *New York World* declared that "the book is a nearly flawless synthesis of the general and the particular" and compared favorably Young's understanding of Italy with that of Henry James and Nathaniel Hawthorne.[7] (A comparison with William Dean

Howells would have been more pertinent.) In the *New York Times,* Mary Siegrist wrote that "these genial sketches" are "a gesture, an atmosphere, a remembrance and an evocation of beautiful things. There is room in them for poetry and meditation and laughter."[8] The volume enhanced Young's literary reputation and rewarded Scribner's financially.

Glamour

In May 1924 Young approached Perkins about a plan for a second book of drama criticism.[9] The work was plainly modeled after *The Flower in Drama.* Comprised mainly of articles reworked from the *North American Review,* the *New Republic, Vanity Fair,* and *Theatre Arts,* the volume was to be divided into sections entitled "Visitors," "The Prompt Book," "Letters from Dead Actors," "Duse," and "Creative Criticism." Young planned to call it "Dionysos' Garland," a title he had already used for an article in the *North American Review* dealing with the 1921–22 theatrical season.

At the suggestion of Sherwood Anderson, however, Young changed the title to *Glamour;* and, as the work developed, he altered its contents. He shifted the essay on "Duse" from the later part of the book to the opening. The change was appropriate because the new arrangement implied a continuity with *The Flower in Drama,* which had concluded with a piece on Duse, and because it called attention to her recent tragic death in Pittsburgh on 23 April 1924. In the place originally planned for the Duse material, Young used an essay entitled "The Art of Directing." He also changed the title of the final chapter from "Creative Criticism" to "Sophocles' Guest."

By beginning his book with three chapters devoted to "Visitors," Young emphasized the importance of national traditions in acting. Eleonora Duse, whom Young considered the finest dramatic artist he had ever seen, had begun her final tour of the United States on 29 October 1923, at the Metropolitan Opera House in Ibsen's *The Lady from the Sea.* Upon her arrival, Young, who had written glowing tributes to her in the *New Republic, The Flower in Drama,* and elsewhere, had been delightfully surprised to receive a telegram from her asking him to visit her. In the essay in *Glamour,* derived in part from this

interview and his earlier articles about her, Young tries to identify the qualities that made her preeminent and to associate
her with the Italian national character. To those who had read
Young's earlier accounts of her, the essay in *Glamour* could
scarcely escape being repetitious. The same comment could be
made about the chapters on "Madame Sorel" and "The Moscow
Art Theatre" and, for that matter, about the remainder of the
book, since very little of its contents had not already appeared
in periodicals. The genuine merit of the volume lies in Young's
rearrangements and additions to produce a unified treatise upon
the art of the theatre with particular emphasis upon acting.

Eleonora Duse was the living embodiment of Stark Young's
ideals of the theatre. He conceded that she might not have
been the greatest actress, but he insisted that she was the greatest
artist. She combined the inner and emotional faculties that
Young demanded of the supreme artist with an almost instinctive
ability to use her body, particularly her face, to project her
feelings and response to dramatic situations. At the very beginning of his chapter, he summarized his judgment of her by
saying that "more than any other [actor] Duse brought to the
art of acting the largest and most poignant idea, the profoundest
sensitivity, the deepest and most exquisite response to experience. Of all the people in the theatre she had most in common
with great poetry, great joy and sorrow and beauty, great living"
(3). Duse was never the overpowering actress that Sarah Bernhardt was; but though she could be brilliant and often dazzling,
the French actress could project only a limited range of ideas
and emotions. What Duse had that surpassed all others was
essentially, for Young, character, an inner purity, a greatness
of mind, an understanding of suffering, and the "quintessence
of the woman" (30). At the same time, she was profoundly
Italian; she had about her something of the Italian land and
the small Italian towns that had cultivated beauty, freedom, and
naturalness. But most of all, for Young, Duse's supreme quality
was her "response to life." She accorded fully with his conviction
that to be a great artist one must possess inner greatness as a
person. As he wrote, "in Duse of all artists people most felt
the thing they most respond to in all living, an infinity of tragic
wonder and tenderness" (31). Many readers considered the
chapter on Duse the finest in the volume. John Mason Brown,

himself an able critic, for example, thought it "extraordinary" and added that Young had unraveled and defined the most intangible qualities of her art and brought her "back to life in prose of amazing beauty."[10]

Young's choice of the visits of Cécile Sorel and the Moscow Art Theatre gave him opportunities to discuss the French and Russian national theatres. He thought that in a second rank actress like Sorel the character of the French tradition showed more plainly than it would have in an actress of Sarah Bernhardt's or Gabrielle Réjane's caliber. Using Madame Sorel's acting in Dumas's *le Demi-Monde* as his point of departure, Young conceded that she had nothing of the eloquence of Mounet Sully, none of the grand style, and none of the profound resonance and ease of action found in the Comédie Française at its best. But both Madame Sorel and the Dumas play did exhibit the urban quality of French drama. The French tradition, wrote Young, is "sophisticated rather than inspired" (39), an art that "depends on no illusion" (40), an art an audience can accept without believing in it. Young concluded that French drama is an art preeminently social and civilized but limited because it cannot penetrate the ultimate reaches of human experience. Its great advantage is that it allows for the development of a style as a medium in which "heightened artifice, intelligence, and emotional reality are all at one and the same time apparent" (46). (Young considered the best "style" one in which its elements were inevitable but not apparent.)

Young's two essays—"The Moscow Art Theatre" and "Many Gods"—that form the nucleus of the chapter in *Glamour* dealing with the visit of the Russian company to New York have already been discussed.[11] Although he expanded the material, his main argument about the inadequacy of exact realism in the handling of historical themes remained unchanged. The realistic method was more successful in the treatment of Chekhov, in whose work Young saw a likeness to that of Shakespeare. "Out of this modern and realistic art," wrote Young, "I got something of the same thing that comes off from Shakespeare: the tragic excitement, the vivacity and pathetic beauty, the baffling logic of emotion, the thrill that arises from a sense of truth" (60). Young also reaffirmed the significance of the Russians' visit for the development of American actors. Although this chapter fitted easily into the section entitled "Visitors," it contained little that was new.

In the second major division of *Glamour,* Young included several essays under the umbrella heading "The Prompt Book," a repetition of a title he had used in *The Flower in Drama* and earlier in the *New Republic.* Although these chapters, which are virtual reprints of articles he had written for *Theatre Arts,* ostensibly deal with acting, they contain many of Young's concepts of arts and artists. The most important is "Seeing the Point."

Young's theory of art arises from the major premise that the most enduring art contains "a great central pattern of idea and significance" (70) expressed in terms of the artist's medium. Young illustrates this concept by examples drawn from music, painting, poetry, architecture, and the drama. In each instance, the *idea* or "essential quality" becomes the *sine qua non* of the art, but of almost equal importance is his demand that the idea be translated into the component elements of the particular medium through which the artist expresses his idea. In terms of drama (Young includes both the play as written by the playwright and its production), he insists that every element contribute to the realization of the central idea—acting, costuming, scene design, lighting, and whatever else may be involved in the production. "In all arts," asserted Young, "the elements of beauty, style, and purity have at bottom a pressing relation to the perception of the essential quality [or idea]," and "all beauty derives from unity in its essential character" (76). In his insistence upon unity, the subordination of all dramatic components to the realization of the central idea, Young's position seems close to Coleridge's principle of organicism in art.

Young's remarks about style further explain his concept of art. In defining style, he understands two meanings. Style, in terms of a painter or an actor, refers to a certain heightening or added elaboration of the essential idea. It is not so much the idea itself as it is the luster added by the artist (presumably in the drama by both the playwright and the actor but also by other components of the production). In a larger sense, however, style "is the man," the medium by which the idea finds expression, "what appears between the content of a work of art and its appearance in a form" (77). Complete style, concludes Young, is attained only when the idea is translated or infused into every part. In minor artists, style, that is, the translation of the idea or essential characteristic, appears only in this or that part. As an illustration, Young mentions a sculpture of a Greek girl with fauns; all the parts of the work are early Greek except the girl's hands, ankles, and feet, which are modern. In them the idea that dominated the work never found expression in the style.

In Young's aesthetic the function of the critic is to perceive the idea, essential quality, or characteristic element underlying a work of art. He abstracts this idea or quality from the elements of its expression, "carries it to some ideal completion, and then judges the work of art by this ideal, by the extent to which this complete realization of its idea is achieved" (85). In this sentence Young has stated the basis of his drama criticism. As a critic, he sought to identify the central idea or "point" of a play and then to judge it and its production by the degree to which each component element contributed to its realization. In almost all of his drama reviews, he compared what he saw and heard in the theatre with an image in his mind of what ideally should have been. One must not forget, however, that Young demanded also that the idea have "significance," that is, that it have a meaningful relation to the life of man.

The apparent simplicity of Young's explanation of the critic's function somewhat veils the complexity of his own critical processes. On his terms, "seeing the point" and judging the translation of the "point" into the elements of style require a finely tuned aesthetic sensitivity and a far-reaching knowledge of philosophy, literature, history, and the other artistic disciplines involved in drama productions. Young's criticism is often impressionistic in that it depends upon his own emotional and intellectual responses to a given scene, act, or entire play. That he is more often right than wrong attests to the sharpness of his critical faculties. Perhaps Young as critic is most aptly characterized as the artist in the role of critic.

Young continued the application of his aesthetic criteria in the five "Letters from Dead Actors," the section of *Glamour* most popular with contemporary readers. Revised and expanded from the original series that had appeared in *Vanity Fair,* they follow Young's frequent practice of comparing performances current on Broadway with acting in earlier schools abroad. In the letter from Rachel (Elisa Félix, 1820–58) to Pauline Lord, Young compares the French classical tradition of acting with that of modern realism. Young believes that an actor can never achieve greatness in either style until he has learned to find the idea or truth in his material and attained the expertness with which to convey it to his audience. Maddalena Raffi (La Corallina), an Italian actress of the eighteenth century, insists that primarily the play of the mind makes great acting and complains that the American theatre is all too often satisfied with infantile, sentimental comedy. Doris Keane, whose acting in Edward Sheldon's *Romance* was "right," has the wit to perform comedy with distinction. In the letter from David Garrick (1717–79) to John Barrymore, Young's main point is that the essence of Hamlet is that men can never understand fully the complexities of his character. In acting the role, Barrymore needs to portray Hamlet as a man of complex suffering, not as an easily understood, uncomplicated man, too simple, too easily digested. For the fourth letter, Young chose Molly Nelson, an American actress who performed with great talent in the Deep South, especially in New Orleans, but never was seen by anyone who could have recognized her merits and brought her to New York. She writes to Margalo Gillmore, whose performance as Consuelo in Andreyev's *He Who Gets Slapped,* Molly thinks, falls short of conveying the idea of eternal beauty embodied in the role. Molly, who never has the chance that fortune gives Margalo, is one of those left to waste, unarrived anywhere. In the final letter, Mlle Jeanne Beauval (1648–1720) laments the lack of great acting on the modern stage: the actors have become respectable ladies and gentlemen, but as a group they include few if any genuine artists.

Having been mainly concerned in the previous sections of *Glamour* with aesthetics and the art of acting, Young progressed to a discussion of the place of the director in the theatre. For Young, directing, like acting, is an art, since the director, like the painter painting a landscape, takes his material (the written play or the landscape) and re-creates or restates it in terms of his medium (the theatre or the painting). Young distinguishes two types of directors: the virtuoso who by radically translating the play into his own terms makes it his own and the director who subordinates his own responses in order to carry out the intentions of the dramatist. Both kinds of directors are artists, since a play can no more be directed as it was written than a landscape can be painted as it actually is. Most contemporary directors, asserts Young, fall somewhere between these two extremes.

A good director must study a play as an orchestral director examines a symphony. He must discover its essential idea and determine where to place emphasis. The speed, the vocal tone of the actors, and the tempo of their voices all rest upon a musical base. The director must understand that the length, the beat, and the duration of the speeches are parts related to its idea. Likewise, he must discover what visual qualities will best express the essential idea of any given scene. He must also consider the relationship between the play and the audience, since the theatre, an essentially impure medium, consists not only of what takes place on stage but also the reactions of the audience. Young observes that revivals of plays present different problems. *Macbeth,* for example, must be restated in every revival and, in fact, in every performance. If a director could discover every facet of the first production of *Macbeth* and could reproduce it exactly, he would not necessarily convey to the contemporary audience the life of the play.

Of crucial importance to the successful direction of a play is the relationship of the director to the actor. Some directors—Young seems to be talking about the virtuoso type—wholly dominate every aspect of the production. They instruct the actor how to speak each line, the tempo, the time between speeches, the gestures—every detail. Such a director often makes the actor into an imitation of himself. Other directors seek to employ good actors and allow them to determine all of these matters. Young believes that this method leads to laziness on the part of the director and weak dramatic productions. The ideal director would combine elements of both methods.

In a comment that reflects his experience in directing *Welded* and *The Failures,* Young observes that it ought to be true that the more a director can utilize the actor's own concept of a role and his own artistic abilities the better the performance. The director thus brings the actor's own truth to enhance the larger truth that the director seeks to express. In *The Failures,* for example, a black man suddenly discovers a corpse and cries aloud. As director, Young would allow the actor first to make this cry himself, expressing his own kind of emotion, rather than give him a cry to imitate. In other words, the director should respect the integrity of the actor's own art. Young would have agreed, however, that poor actors would need the coaching of the director.

"Sophocles' Guest," the concluding section of *Glamour*, reprinted from the *North American Review,* relates to the theatre primarily because it begins with a young man's attendance at a revival of Sophocles' *Oedipus Rex* in Athens. The classical drama prompts the young man, who may be a reflection of Young himself, to examine the Greek attitude toward life in terms of the modern world. The youth finds that for Sophocles and the Greeks, the important elements in life are forms (ideas, qualities) that are produced by forces that give them continuity. To contemplate these forces and their wise application to life is more important than to examine the private experiences of individuals. The young man is struck with the difference between this Greek approach to life and the modern exaltation of the unique personality. Sophocles made his characters types, since in his view man is most himself when he is most universal, that is, universal "by some more or less completion in himself of ideas, enduring conceptions, parallels of the continuous in human experience." What moves him in the characters of Sophocles' play is "only certain living ideas, permanent forces in human living, passion, wisdom, anger, heredity, beauty" (202). Finally, the young man understands that these ideas, forms, and qualities are the only permanent elements of human life. Were he to think of God, he would image Him as some Ultimate Mind by which all things could be perceived. God would then be "a kind of antiphonal radiance of all things among themselves, by which alone their truth appears" (208). In choosing to conclude *Glamour* with this somewhat Platonic statement and acceptance of what he interpreted as the Greek approach to life, Young was expressing a philosophical attitude that influenced his drama criticism. In this respect, "Sophocles' Guest" is an appropriate ending for the volume. (The passage also reveals how far Young had departed from the Protestant theological beliefs of his youth.)

While teaching at Amherst, Young wrote short plays to amuse the children of President Meiklejohn. They became popular in Amherst with other children ages five to ten. Early in January 1925, Young offered thirteen of these pieces to Perkins, but the educational department at Scribner's declined them. Young was convinced of their appeal when read aloud to children either as short stories or fairy tales. Late in 1925, Henry Holt and Company brought them out as *Sweet Times and The Blue Policeman,* dedicated to Young's nephew, Stark Young Robertson. The volume proved a successful venture and remained on Holt's list for almost a decade.

Theatre Practice

Scribner's educational department seems to have voiced no objections to Young's *Theatre Practice.* [12] Essentially this volume consists of a selection of essays about acting taken from *The Flower in Drama* and *Glamour.* To them Young added, with slight revisions, chapters on "Character Acting" and "Wearing Costumes," which had originally been published in *Theatre Arts.* The series of study questions placed at the end of each chapter gives the work an appearance of a textbook on acting. To those who had read Young's earlier work, *Theatre Practice* must have seemed repetitious, although it does bring together a considerable number of his theories about acting. The unifying element of *Theatre Practice* is Young's basic premise that acting is one— and probably the most important—of the component arts that together comprise theatre.

In "Character Acting," Young distinguishes two kinds of acting. The first, represented by such supreme artists as Duse, Bernhardt, and Grasso, arises from within the actor himself as he strives to present the inner feelings of the persons he represents. The second type, "character acting," depends largely upon the actor's mimicry and external details; examples would include tramps, misers, irate fathers, Irishmen, and "cranky old ladies." As examples of gifted "character" actors, Young mentions Haidee Wright, Ouspenskaya, David Warfield, George Arliss, and Roland Young. Curiously, he makes no mention of Charlie Chaplin in either group. Although Young asserts that "to be set down as a character actor has nothing in it to chagrin a player" and recalls that in the past supreme artists have played all types of roles with equal success, clearly Young gives character acting a second rank. Many actors who lack "the magnetism, the control, the direct instinct or whatever it is that would carry their direct selves over the footlights" (78) might perform very well in character parts.

Character acting might also help to free the actor from the defects of the mistaken but prevalent concepts of acting as "pretty much a matter of exhibitionism" and as a "natural happening" (81). The nature of acting and of all other arts rests upon the same basis. In all of them, Young declares, "the method, the form, the style, proceeds from the content, the idea to be expressed." Thus, naturalism in acting relates not to what the actor feels but to the nature of what he is to express. "A form is the natural body of the idea that it conveys" (83), repeats Young. Character acting, like scales for the musician or drawing nudes for the painter, avoids sheer exhibitionism by taking the actor outside of himself. It demands an outline that is not the actor's own but that must be achieved by external as well as internal means. Character acting may enable the actor to study his art more objectively, and it may diminish "some of the nonsense, now so current, about art as inspiration, as the visitation of angels and nervous fits, as pure impulse, cosmic creation, or divinely abysmal egotism" (85). Finally, character work helps the actor to learn imitation, skill in handling external detail, and mimicry; and it may assist him in cultivating the sense of wit or poetry.

In "Wearing Costumes," Young recalls his discussion in *Glamour* of "Seeing the Point." Ideally, writes Young, a costume is a "visual description" of what the actor's speeches and gestures express in words and actions. Seeing the point here consists of an actor perceiving the essential or characteristic quality of a costume and translating this quality into the actor's own body. Costumes, like other components of the theatre art, become art when "clothes are translated into something which they were not before, and have added to them something that was not there before" (95). Once more, Young makes the analogy with painting. Just as Velasquez added something to the "original clothes" in his painting, so the costume designer translates the original clothes into theatrical terms. Costumes thus created interpret or create a dramatic mood. Beginning with the literal clothes, the artist-designer may "extend a line here or heighten a quality there; he will intensify a tone, he will eliminate and underscore, he will do whatever is necessary to force the costume to say the dramatic thing that is necessary to the moment." His goal is "the expression of an idea in stage garments" (97).

In designing period or historical costumes, the artist-designer deals in part with an actuality already established, but he must also express the quality of a given epoch. The perfect historical costume must render the characteristic essence of the past society, including its social ideas, its standards of taste, and its philosophy of art and life. As examples, Young compares Spanish costumes in the time of Philip IV and those expressed in the paintings of Velasquez. In wearing costumes, the actor must add something of his own to what the artist-designer has created and must conform his acting to the qualities represented in the costume.

Ideally, acting and costuming should be mutually supportive. When they are not, the production suffers. As an example, Young recalls a young actress in the role of Mrs. Candour in Sheridan's *The School for Scandal.* The actress in one scene exited hanging on the arms of two gentlemen, "laughing merrily and archly." She should have known from her costume, even from the powder in her hair, that such a manner was not possible. She had no concept of what her clothes expressed. In Young's terms, she did not "wear" her eighteenth-century costume. The point her clothes made was lost upon her.

In his drama criticism for the *New Republic* and elsewhere, Young frequently deals with the contribution of costumes to play productions, and often he calls attention not only to the work of the artist-designer but also to the actor's ability to wear his costume effectively. Perhaps nowhere, however, does he summarize his position more effectively than in the closing portion of this essay, when he writes: "Just as the actor's being fills his body, which in turn expresses it, so the actor, himself, body and being, fills his costume, which expresses him or what, during the time he has it on, he must be. This that he must be while he has on the costume derives from his translation of it into his own mood; from this translation derives the idea that the costume provides a body for, and through the idea within it this costume-body is alive" (105).

To reviewers who complained that Young compiled his *The-*

atre Practice from *The Flower in Drama* and *Glamour,* he could have replied that in view of the educational purpose of the work and his intention of covering the arts of the theatre, a rephrasing of what he had already written was hardly necessary. He knew too that what he presented was not often found in books on the drama designed for students. The two entirely new chapters on "Character Acting" and "Wearing Costumes" extend the scope of the volume; and the questions at the end of each chapter invite the reader to explore for himself the implications of what Young has written. In one respect, however, Young failed to cover all of the essential areas; his volume lacks a discussion of theatre decor, an omission that he would correct in his next volume.

The Theater

Young's fourth volume of essays on the arts of the theatre appeared as a part of George H. Doran's Modern Readers' Bookshelf, a publisher's series designed to present "simple, short, authoritative" discussions of contemporary subjects.[13] While Young's essays in *The Theater* can hardly be called "simple," they offer a clear statement of his major ideas. Young himself felt that *The Theater* was "one of the most solid things I have worked out."[14] Although in preparing the volume he reworked essays that he had earlier published in periodicals, much of it represented new writing. He completed the manuscript in February 1927 and dedicated the volume to Edward Sheldon, author of *Romance,* the play that brought fame to Doris Keane. In 1958 Hill and Wang reissued the book in paperback with a dedication to Eric Bentley, a leading contemporary critic whose work Young greatly admired.

A person familiar with Young's other volumes of drama criticism would encounter in *The Theater* restatements and, at times, elaborations of his earlier principles. For this reason, the book becomes a convenient summary of his drama criticism. Young never tired of repeating his major premise that the essence of art is the translation of one thing (idea, quality) in terms of another medium so that something appears that was not there before. In other words, art is an idea or quality that the artist has added to nature. Young illustrates this premise in terms

of various arts, but especially music, architecture, painting, poetry, and dance. Theatre is at once an art and the most complex
of arts, because it consists of a number of widely differing medi-
ums, including those of the dramatist, director, actors, designer,
and musician, all of whom are artists working in different arts.
Unlike the other arts, the theatre is "impure," since many arts
intervene between the artist's (dramatist's) idea and the expression of it. At its best, the theatre is a complex of these arts
working in harmony to express an idea. In an ideal situation,
the dramatist would write and direct his own play, supported
by actors able to express completely his idea and by an artist-
designer whose settings and costumes would bring the production to perfection. No one knew better than Stark Young that
such a combination would never occur in practice, but it represents the ultimate standard by which the perceptive and sensitive
critic could and should determine the merits and defects of a
production.

Although he is inclined to emphasize the arts that intervene
between the playwright's written words and their realization
on the stage, Young considers the play itself the most important
element of the theatre. "A play," writes Young, "is a piece
of literature about a section of life written in such a way that
it will go over the footlights, in such a way that what it has to
say it can say in the theater" (68). Thus, a piece of writing
may be dramatic and yet not a play; the question of whether
it is a play or not rests solely upon "the relation between the
idea and the medium" (69). The play contributes the essential
idea on which its theatrical production is built, and it may have
permanent value as literature even when not expressed wholly
in theatrical terms. But in theatre, in Young's sense, a great
deal must be added to the words of the script before they can
pass from literature into theatre art, and in each production—
and performance—the play is re-created or translated into new
terms. Among those added elements Young includes "the sound
of the actor's voice" and "the time values that he creates" in
speaking, "the stage spaces and the positions of the persons
on it with regard to each other, the lights, the scene itself"
(41), and the audience. A large portion of *The Theater* relates
to the intervening arts that translate the words of the playwright
into theatre art.

Of all the theatre arts that transform the script into theatre, the actor's art is the most important. In both *The Flower in Drama* and *Glamour,* Young writes a great deal about acting. In *The Theater,* he summarizes his understanding of the actor's contribution by distinguishing five aspects of the acting medium: theatricality, or the ability to project himself over the footlights; his natural assets, including his body, voice, and presence; his time sense, that is, his timing, rhythm, and grasp of cues; his visual motion or sense of movement and ability to wear costumes effectively; and his mimetic gift. Young reaffirms his conviction that the actor is never the character he plays but always himself, and he need not feel the emotion he portrays. He needs to learn the language of the theatre—technique. He must also grasp the dramatist's idea in the play; and through the creation of the idea into acting form, he "achieves a work of art, complete in itself and free of its material" (118). Only through "his idea does the actor know his share in the whole work of theater art that he serves; the rest of him is merely used by the director and the dramatist" (120).

Just as the orchestral conductor grasps a symphony or musical piece in its entirety and deduces from it the composer's idea, the play director must see the play as a whole and extract from it the essential idea of the dramatist. To translate this idea into theatrical terms, the director must know where to place emphasis, what parts require subordination, and when a given speech is crucial to the main plot or theme. Keeping the idea in mind, the director must also determine what part of the production will depend upon acting, the dialogue, time values, visual rhythm, and decor. He can force the entire production into a reflection of himself, or he can give wide latitude to the component parts; in each instance he acts at his peril. Young seems to favor a combination of the two approaches, since most actors need the director's assistance. Together they are the most important persons in the production; generally speaking, they are ahead of the artist-designer responsible for the decor.

In his earlier books on the theatre, Young occasionally mentions the contribution of the artist-designer to the translation of the dramatist's play into the art of the theatre. In particular, he praises the work of his friend and close associate Robert Edmond Jones, as well as the effects created by Max Eastman and Gordon Craig; but except for costume design, which he included in decor, he says little about the contribution and problems of the artist-designer. In *The Theater,* Young devotes an entire chapter to this subject.

In Young's criticism decor is viewed as a highly individualistic creation of a single artist (except in costuming where the actor is involved). Its object, writes Young, is "to create something that justifies itself by expressing what nothing else could quite express" (144). In other words, the idea has found its own proper form. A mediocre designer may create a decor neither pointedly inappropriate nor intrusive, and such a decor may neither harm nor help a production. The realistic drama of modern times, however, Young believes is prone to foster extremes. Here the object is to translate "the real material, such as a room or a scene, into the quality of the play" (140). Often the translation does not take place, and the result is a kind of photography which is not art at all. Young does not object to realistic decor as such and cites the perfect setting that the Moscow Art Theatre created for Chekhov's *The Cherry Orchard.* Here the setting became "cousin to the play" (141). On the other hand, the designer may go to the extreme of symbolism and allegory and sink to "mere obvious allegory and platitudes of stylization" (142). The difficulty with symbols and stylization is often that they are not used with imagination. "Nothing is more obvious than symbolism when it is poor or perfunctory" (144). Young concludes his discussion by asserting that there is no "right way" in decor. The test is whether something has been created that supports and enhances the idea sought by the other component arts. If it does, the decor belongs to the art of the theatre.

Throughout his drama criticism Stark Young is disturbed at the movement toward realism that he feels characterizes American theatre of the twentieth century. Historically he knew that eighteenth-century neoclassicism had broken down into romantic naturalism. The formal garden became a "pretty chaos" and painters sought "artlessness and narrative likeness." Even the poets sought to become "artless." In modern times much has been done "to break down such limitations in the theory of these arts," but the art of the theatre has moved more slowly. In America the theatre still seeks "resemblance, production, photography" (159–60). Young is convinced that realism in the theatre has dangerous limitations.

Young defines realism as a "method in which outer details, and only outer details, . . . are employed to express what the artist wishes to express" (160). He denies that realism presents "life as it is," because there is no "isness to life." Like any other method in art, realism "selects, arranges, breathes into its material the idea that will preserve it from universal welter and chaos" (161). The theory has encouraged and flattered those who hold the "democratic" approach to art, that is, those who believe that everyman or anyman, since he "naturally" knows things as they are, can properly judge art in the theatre. He has only to compare what he sees in the theatre with the "daily surface displayed to his eyes and ears," not to "life abundant, everlasting, and mysterious" (164). For Young the fallacy is that the "average man" does not see with precision and has little or no sense of tradition or training in taste. Realism has dulled his appreciation and narrowed his understanding of art while giving critical approval to his uninformed judgments.

Young acknowledges that there can be great realism in the theatre, but he warns against confusing the theatre with reality. The theatre is an art, just as painting, music, and architecture are arts. The function of the theatre is "to exalt, amuse, clarify and enrich our lives, to hold up to us the splendor and measure of time and memory against which our lives, in their greatness, meanness, proportion and absurdity, are led" (181). The test of a theatrical work of art is not the number of persons in the audience who understand it, though the greatest art has a wide appeal. Rather, concludes Young, the test is that, to those who do comprehend it, "its meaning is lofty and significant" (182).

For more than twenty years, Stark Young wrote brilliantly about the art of the theatre, but with the exception of a single volume published at the very end of his career as a critic he published no additional books of drama criticism. His opposition to realism or naturalism in the theatre increased as American dramatists and their politically liberal critics came to favor sociological or propagandistic plays in the 1930s. Young's early enthusiasm, strengthened by the new developments in the theatre, especially the work of the Moscow Art Theatre and the Provincetown group, began to fade as he saw Broadway's commercialism

submerge the art of men like Robert Edmond Jones, Kenneth
Macgowan, and Max Eastman. Young remained a unique phenomenon, the only important critic of his time (with the possible
exception of George Jean Nathan) consistently to measure
Broadway against the great achievements of drama in the past.
Undoubtedly, his judgments were colored by his Southern outlook, but the precise extent of that influence cannot be measured.
Certainly his dedication to the values of timeless art and beauty
and their significance for the life of the individual was compatible
with his preference for the Southern attitudes that he was already
beginning to express in fiction.

Chapter Five

Mississippi Fiction

Early in 1926, while writing reviews for the *New York Times*, polishing the manuscript of *Theatre Practice*, and completing *Encaustics* (a volume of essays taken largely from material published earlier in the *New Republic*), Stark Young announced to Maxwell Perkins that his "end" of *Heaven Trees*, his first novel, was "about done."[1] *Heaven Trees*, which Scribner's published in the fall of that year, would be followed by *The Torches Flare* (1928), *River House* (1929), Young's essay in *I'll Take My Stand* (1930), and *So Red the Rose* (1934). Taken with the play *The Colonnade*, which has been previously discussed, *The Street of the Islands* (1930), and *Feliciana* (1935), these volumes, mostly fiction, form, as Donald Davidson has suggested, an "organic unity, whose focus is chiefly upon the South."[2] They apply, continues Davidson, "the artistic principles and moral philosophy" that undergird his drama criticism and infuse his final book, the autobiographical *The Pavilion* (1951). Through them Stark Young became a leader in the movement for a renaissance in Southern literature.

Heaven Trees

From the time Stark Young began to work on *Heaven Trees* in the summer of 1923 to the middle of May 1926, when he finished reading the page proofs, he had completed at least three and perhaps four drafts of the manuscript.[3] In June 1923 he wrote Perkins that he was making notes for a novel that he wanted to have "a real distinction and quality and a difference."[4] He would work on it during the summer in Texas. By that fall he could show some progress, enough for the publication of a chapter called "My Uncle's House" in the *New Republic* (23 October 1923). In the spring of 1925 he finished another draft; but, after discussions with Perkins, Young made substantial alterations in the general plan of the work. In the summer of that year he visited briefly in Como and Oxford, where his aging father's health was rapidly deteriorating.

A few months later Dr. Young died, and Young returned to Mississippi for the funeral. Two years earlier, in writing *The Colonnade,* he had grasped the literary potential of the Southern material. Now in these unhappy circumstances, as he renewed friendships and visited the places he had known in boyhood, Young found his feelings for Southern people and Southern ways of living sharpened. Ever since moving to New York, he had been aware of the contrasts between life in Como and life in the metropolitan city. Urban living lacked the beauty and simplicity that he had known in the South. As early as the summer of 1922, Young had written about the unfeeling shallowness of New Yorkers. After seeing two young women on a subway, Young remarked: "How strangely empty the two women's faces were! You see them repeated in swarms on New York streets and in the trains everywhere. Faces empty though amiably hard; the faces of people who want nothing very much. Faces that are active, competent for the ends desired . . . but without any depth after all, untouched by things for which men have died. . . . In them humanity is visibly reduced to its platitude."⁵ New York, of course, had its advantages—plays, symphony orchestras, ballets, museums, libraries, publishing houses—cultural facilities that for Young were a necessity. But it lacked the human and poetic elements, the closeness to nature, that Young also required.

The return to the South renewed Young's desire to finish his novel. "I set to work on my book again," wrote Young. "I took the old Tait house for my setting, and the people of the book are partly real, partly created. . . . I put them . . . back there in the fifties [1850s], and into these imaginary figures of them I have tried to put some of the qualities and some of the fragrance of their spirits as I myself knew them. . . . If I could make that old life and those people seem gentle and kind, and give to them a certain distinction as well, a certain way of life that was charming and also intelligent, that was generous and warm and direct, I should be happy indeed." Young sought to deal not only with the people but also with the poetry and beauty of the Southern land. As he said, he wanted to give "to my picture of that Southern country a certain poetry and abundance, . . . a hint of those summer nights, of those flowers and spring rains and that sound of children playing in the quarters, of water in a fountain and of the life of children playing in a garden with the little darky friends."[6]

The novel, as published by Scribner's, may best be described as an idealization of actuality. The places, events, and characters are solidly based upon the reality of Young's boyhood. The title offers a good example of his method. In keeping with his use of "Flower House" in *The Colonnade,* Young named the focal point of his novel, the plantation and mansion, Heaven Trees. He had in mind two unusually large "heaven trees" said to have been planted by the McGehee family in the pioneer days of Panola County. An Asiatic tree naturalized in America because of its beauty, shade, and resistance to smoke, heaven trees, often called "trees of the Gods," were not common in north Mississippi. In Young's novel, the name not only suggests the actual trees and the beauty of nature but also the quality of life in the South.

Young located Heaven Trees in Panola County near the old town of Panola, an Indian word meaning cotton. Historically, the county was established in 1836 from lands ceded by the Chickasaw Indians at the treaty of Pontotoc (1832). Incorporated in 1840, Panola reached its maximum population of about 1,000 persons in 1850. In 1856, two years after the only specific date mentioned in Young's novel, the Mississippi and Tennessee railroad was built through Panola County by Colonel Hugh McGehee, Dr. George Tait, Frank White, and others. It passed about a mile east of Panola. The Reverend J. W. Bates, a popular Methodist minister, donated land as a site for the depot. In *Heaven Trees* Bates appears as Parson Bates, a friend of Dr. George Clay and a part-time railroad conductor. The town that resulted from the construction of the railroad was called Batesville, and, eventually, the buildings at old Panola were placed on rollers and moved to Batesville.

Young knew, of course, that the railroad brought about the extinction of Panola, though it also brought industry and commerce to the area. Young places the time of his novel in the mid-1850s, when Panola had little commerce or industry. Actually, when the Mississippi and Tennessee railroad reached Como, about twelve miles north of Batesville, Dr. George Tait donated the land for the depot with the understanding that there would be no commercial buildings in the town. For the purposes of his novel, Young attributes the donation of the land and the stipulation of "no town" to Dr. Clay and changes the town from Como to Panola. Both the selection of the extinct town of Panola and the prohibition of shops, stores, and other commercial enterprises contribute to Young's intention to place his novel in an area where there was no industry or commerce. He wanted Heaven Trees to be an agrarian community.

Young knew that his relatives and friends in Mississippi would recognize such place names as Panola, Sardis, Longtown, Senatobia, and Oxford. They would also identify the brick church at Fredonia, a short distance east of Como, with its plaster columns across the front porch, leaded windows, "the black beams and wainscoting, and the black pews." As a young boy, Young had been baptized there and formally received into the congregation. *Heaven Trees,* however, is not merely a book about the places Young had known in Mississippi; it is, as he said, "about my family."[7] He made no secret of the fact that "walking through these pages, either singly or two or three mixed into one character, [are] some of the McGehees and Wallaces and Taits and Dandridges, my Uncle Hugh McGehee, Uncle George Tait, Miss Mary Cherry, Grandfather McGehee and Uncle Shelton, Solomon Tait, Parson Bates and others whom we have always known or heard of."[8] There were persons in Como who disapproved Young's use of the names of actual persons and disliked the stories he told about them; but he faced no such outcry as Thomas Wolfe encountered in Asheville after the publication of *Look Homeward, Angel* three years later.

Heaven Trees is a loosely organized collection of stories, most of which could have been published, as several were, by themselves. Adopting a technique similar to that William Faulkner would use in 1938 for *The Unvanquished,* Young tells the stories through a narrator, Hugh Stark, who acts as the author's voice. In life, Hugh Stark was the son of the Reverend Stephen Gilbert Stark and Caroline Charlotte McGehee; he was, of course, Young's uncle and his mother's brother. Hugh Stark died as a child. In fiction, Hugh Stark, the narrator, is an elderly man; he constantly reminds the reader of his position in the book by such phrases as "I recall," "I suppose," "I can remember," "the memory I have," "a long way back now seems," and "only long afterward." The device enables Young to place the time of the novel in the mid-1850s, thereby avoiding the Civil War, and to make his own judgments upon the characters and events.

With minor exceptions the other fictional members of the McGehee family correspond to actuality. The fictional Dr. George Clay, the head of the family at Heaven Trees, was modeled primarily upon Dr. George Tait. Both in the novel and in life, each man was married twice, first to Ann McGehee—the sister of Caroline Charlotte McGehee—and second to Martha Stark (Boardman), who was also married twice. Martha Stark Boardman, whose first husband was a schoolmaster in Vermont, was the sister of the Reverend Stephen Gilbert Stark, who married Caroline Charlotte McGehee, Ann McGehee's sister. By his first wife, Ann McGehee, Dr. Clay (Tait) had a daughter Georgia; and by her first husband Martha Stark had a son Charles Boardman. Young explains these relationships through his representative Hugh Stark: "Uncle George [Clay-Tait] was my uncle-in-law twice; his first wife, Ann, was my mother's sister, his second wife my father's. Georgia was Uncle George's daughter by his first wife, Charles was Aunt Martha's son by her first husband. Grandfather McGehee was the father of my mother and of Georgia's mother. On my mother's side Georgia was my first cousin, on my father's side Charles was my first cousin" (7). The characters included in this tangle of relationships form only the nucleus of the family at Heaven Trees. In narrating the various incidents, Hugh Stark mentions by name at least a dozen aunts and uncles, almost two dozen cousins, and a bewildering assortment of friends and servants. Hugh Stark explains: "If confusion reigns in these pages . . . it is little wonder; we hardly had it [the relationships] straight ourselves" (7). At first readers of *Heaven Trees* usually try to keep the genealogical ties straight, but gradually they become less and less significant. Young wished the reader to understand that these people belonged to one immense family held together by blood, affection, and tradition. He saw this feature as distinctly Southern, and throughout his subsequent novels he would continue to represent the family as the basis of the good life.[9]

Hugh Stark's memories of life at Heaven Trees form the

substance of the novel. Although the events he recalls are arranged in accordance with the progression of the seasons beginning with April 1853 to May 1854, the anecdotes he tells about
the characters range backward and forward in time. In successive
chapters he recounts the arrival of his Cousin Ellen from Vermont; the arguments at Heaven Trees over such matters as the
Bible, the Constitution, and the proper use of words; the visits
of Mary Cherry; the annual tournament of "knights"; the death
of Cousin Virginia; and the debacle of Grandfather McGehee's
second marriage. Young achieves a measure of unity from these
chronicles through the narrator and the focus upon the family's
activities.

What little there is of suspensive plot arises from the courtship
of Georgia Clay by Charles Boardman and the "Southernizing"
of Ellen Stark. Young seems to have refrained from giving these
two matters very much attention, probably because he did not
wish them to overshadow his emphasis upon the characters and
actions of the family. Hugh Stark, however, does refer repeatedly to Charles's affection for Georgia, his distant cousin by
marriage. Charles is a quiet, sincere, unassuming young man.
His rival, Randall Oliver, is a polished, self-assertive lawyer,
fond of displaying his erudition. Randall's tailors are the fashion-
able Rambeaux and Rambeaux in Memphis. In his latest daguer-
reotype, he wears a coat with a velvet collar, and his ruffled
shirt has a cluster of diamonds in it. Besides his appearance,
Randall's chief social attribute is his voice. After hearing him
sing a melancholy ballad to the accompaniment of Georgia Clay,
who seems greatly impressed, Hugh Stark wonders "just what
Charles had to match against this insinuation and cool security"
(55). At Heaven Trees, Mary Cherry and Parson Bates favor
Randall, while Dr. Clay sides with Charles. A fierce argument
takes place over the merits of each suitor. Because of a misunder-
standing between Charles and Georgia, Randall seems to be
winning. After receiving his proposal, Georgia writes that she
will accept him, but two days later writes again to change her
mind. Thinking Randall did not receive her second letter, Georgia considers eloping with him; but in Memphis the letter acci-
dentally falls out of his portfolio, revealing his concealment of
it. Georgia returns to Heaven Trees and to Charles, whom she
really loves.

The contrast between these two young men illustrates an important Southern value that Young wishes to emphasize. Simplicity and lack of pretense characterize Charles. He makes no attempt to show off his learning or his talents before Georgia. His affection for her is the result of years of association with her through childhood and early schooling. When she leaves for boarding school, Charles leaves for the university at Oxford, "taking with him," as Hugh Stark recalls, "a negro servant, two horses, a gun, and a brace of hunting-hounds" (93). Charles, however, does not neglect the main purpose for going; he is graduated cum laude. Randall by contrast, constantly parades his erudition and endeavors to impress people by his clothes and singing. In the end his deception of Georgia reveals the depth of his pretense and duplicity.

Young employs a similar device to illustrate the differences between persons reared in the North and those reared in the South. Seven or eight years before the arrival of Ellen Stark, Aunt Martha Clay had brought the daughter of a friend in Pittsford, Vermont, to Heaven Trees as governess for Georgia. "A thin-lipped, thin-blooded little spinster" (25), as Hugh Stark remembered her, Miss Jane Pitts lived at Heaven Trees for two years. She disliked the people who seemed to her "morally insincere" (25) and frivolous in their living. She hated the insects that came with the spring season, which she considered "too lavish, too rank with so much vegetation and overripe display" (25–26). Although she eventually returned to Vermont, she remained a very distinct memory at Heaven Trees, "solid, sour, and clear, clear as good vinegar" (26). These were matters that everyone knew, but no one wished to make unkind remarks about her.

Ellen Stark's experience at Heaven Trees is wholly different. She arrives, as Miss Pitts did, in a dress of "spun granite" (83) and with the same grim approach to life that characterized her predecessor. Her mother, Aunt Martha's cousin, had died in childbirth and her father five years later. She lived with her aunt until she died and then kept house for her uncle. He taught her to be "neat, to have a conscience, and to remember that she was a Stark" (22). Hugh Stark recalls her gentle but slightly pinched face and her body that exhibited an "odd sort of solemnity," that is, "a body that seemed to imply moving joyously along in the manner of church suppers and taking its bacchanals on raspberry vinegar" (34).

Ellen has scarcely arrived at Heaven Trees before the charm and beauty of the Southern land begin to work their spell upon her. As she lies in bed, she can see "the yellow rim of the moon above the ledge. It lay on the golden leafage of the wooded lawns like a veil. . . . The great blossoms on the magnolia-trees against the dark were like little moons themselves; and the odor of mimosa, so like the linden-trees at home [in Vermont] in June, came drifting past. A bird was singing like none of the birds at home, wonderfully rich and wild. . . . And there was something everywhere, warm, living, abundant, something exotic and mad, that carried away the senses into a sweet, pagan, terrible world" (79). Everywhere at Heaven Trees she is struck by the contrast between her austere surroundings in Vermont and the beauty, ease, and freshness of the South. She fights her inclination to believe that the laughter, kindness, compliments, and easy conversation are somehow wrong. Standing before the mantel in her bedroom, she feels like "Europa when the divine bull carried her off" (81). Young adds, "Flowers in her hands, in her hair, summer music—and she swept away to where, to what seductions, and what sin? She . . . felt, somehow, as if she were shut up in a music-box without her Bible" (81–82).

For four years, Ellen has been engaged to Henry Gilbert, a Harvard student. In Vermont, because of her engagement, she has refused to go to parties with other men; and when Georgia Clay tells her that in the South girls go to parties with other men up to a week before the wedding invitations are sent, Ellen thinks Southern women promiscuous. Gradually her observations of Georgia and other Southern girls change her opinion.

As the months pass, Ellen grows to love the Southern ways of living. She relaxes and begins to unbend and enjoy life. She soon discards the "spun granite" dresses and discovers the pleasures of new gowns, hats, and tighter corsets that reveal her small, trim waist. She even experiments with rouge. Before the year is out, her waist has been taken in several inches and her shoes are smaller than they were in Vermont. Ellen learns to dance. Most of all, she learns to love the South, its land, its people, and its ways of living. When Aunt Martha and

Dr. Clay suggest that Henry Gilbert, whose cough has grown steadily worse in the New England climate, come to live in Mississippi and manage one of the family's plantations in Tippah County, Ellen is overjoyed at the prospect of a life in the South for Henry, herself, and their children. At the end of the year, this "generous, rich country of the heart, this Southern land" (286) has won her allegiance; and as she contemplates the future, she exclaims, " 'Oh, holy and enchanted life,' . . . the *enchanted* slipping in quite naturally before she knew" (286).

Throughout *Heaven Trees,* Young insisted that the Southern way of life included compassion for the less fortunate, a compassion that often took the form of hospitality. Ellen is impressed by the genuine hospitality extended strangers, friends, and, especially, relatives, however distant. In addition to Ellen herself, the two outstanding examples of the kind of compassionate hospitality that Young knew from his own experience relate to Cousin Virginia and Miss Mary Cherry. Cousin Virginia's husband, "a worthless sort of man" (181), had brought his wife only hardship and wretchedness during their marriage. At his death, his lands were so covered with mortgages and debts of honor that she was left virtually penniless. Although she was of no blood kin to the family at Heaven Trees, she had been a friend. Aunt Martha and Dr. Clay invited Cousin Virginia to stay with them, and for years she remained in their house unable to get out of bed because of a kind of hemorrhage that kept her from standing. Hugh Stark and others in the family saw her only infrequently, but Dr. Clay and Aunt Martha "could not have conceived of Heaven Trees without her" (183). Despite her years of pain, Cousin Virginia never mentioned her illness and remained cheerful, concerned about other members of the family. "It was partly pride if you like," recalls Hugh Stark, "but it was also a manner of insisting on life as an art or at least as a way of grace" (188). The comment expresses the Southern attitude toward life. Cousin Virginia dies as she lived, accepted, admired, and loved by all at Heaven Trees.

Unlike Cousin Virginia, Miss Mary Cherry did not live permanently at Heaven Trees. Rather, she made visits, usually unannounced, sometimes lasting several days and sometimes several months. Stark Young's account of her, in both *Heaven Trees* and *So Red the Rose,* is a "history" of an actual person of that name.[10] Except for a nephew who lived somewhere in Tennessee, she had no family. A large woman, she was neither physically attractive nor popular with the family. She hated Parson Bates, thought Dr. Clay a sot, disapproved of many of the family's ideas and actions, and announced her blunt, unpopular opinions in a loud voice. She made herself at home, called everyone "Sister," and cooked for herself delicacies that she ate at the table without offering them to anyone else. Dr. Clay often told Hugh Stark that Mary Cherry was an "old fool" (232). But when Hugh asked his uncle to explain how Miss Mary Cherry could live in houses for forty years where she had no blood claim, Dr. Clay replied, "She's a lady, you know" (241). No other explanation was ever given. The truth is that Miss Mary Cherry was one of many women in the South who had neither income nor family on whom she could depend. For a large part of her life she existed upon the hospitality and generosity of families like that at Heaven Trees. Young thought these traits characteristic of the Southern way of life.

Important as the children, cousins, and friends who inhabit Heaven Trees are to its daily life, the unquestioned heads of the family are Aunt Martha and Uncle George Clay. Under her management, life on the plantation, from the fields to the bedrooms of the house, moves at an orderly pace. She has successfully reared her children, and she has learned to manage her husband. Understanding Dr. Clay's need for companions and conversation, she encourages his friendship with Parson Bates and tolerates the blunt remarks of Miss Mary Cherry. Her efforts are primarily designed to keep his mental faculties alert and, when possible, to engage him in worthwhile enterprises in the vicinity. Through these means, she seeks to restrain his appetite for alcohol.

Like Stark Young's father, Dr. Clay holds a medical degree from the University of Pennsylvania; but he has long since ceased active practice. Now a wealthy planter, the owner of three hundred slaves, this intellectually active man spends most of his time reading books like Gibbon's history of Rome, arguing with Parson Bates and Miss Mary Cherry, entertaining his friends, and drinking. He has a ready wit, a shrewd insight into character, and a love of the land. But through this generally admirable character Stark Young makes a fundamental criticism of life throughout much of the South. Dr. Clay exhibits little interest in politics; he never mentions the sectional conflict that at the time was already threatening to divide the nation; and he has no real outlet for his creative faculties. Young saw in him an example of what life in the provinces could do to a man of his talents. Miss Mary Cherry was essentially correct when she said that he ought to work. He had nothing compelling to do. Hugh Stark's judgment is that "life wore itself down for him and emptied itself at the same time, he was so warm, so human; and through just that warmth and that humanity he was a very lonely man" (97). Perhaps Hugh Stark gets closer to the truth when he remarks, in words that voice Young's own criticism: "It was partly the provinces again, that remote country and the powerful life in him thwarted and blurred in some ways to a mockery of itself" (66). In Dr. Clay, Young reflected his own situation. Much as he admired life in Panola County, he would have found himself equally stultified had he lived his life there. If Heaven Trees is a kind of Garden of Eden, Young's objection is that there is too little to occupy a gifted man. Despite the beauty of the Southern landscape, the inner charm and goodness of the people, and the relaxed tempo of life, Dr. Clay's existence had little purpose in it. Young saw in him a major weakness in the agrarian life of the South. In creating this idyllic, almost utopian account of the Southern tradition, Young passes lightly over this matter, but he did not forget it when he planned another novel of the South. In *Heaven Trees* his emphasis rests upon the rightness of Dr. Clay's feelings, his *bona natura,* the grace of his way of life.

Although Dr. Clay is a large slaveholder, Young does not make slavery an issue in *Heaven Trees.* Hugh Stark remembers that his uncle's slaves were "well sheltered and well cared for" (275). Only once does Young mention the darker side of slavery. Hugh recalls that one day his Grandfather McGehee came upon a group of slaves being herded by a slave-driver, a brutal Dutchman, who had struck a sickly old woman on the head for failing to keep up with the others. McGehee stopped the march and bought the woman "on the spot"; and when she told him of three slave children who had been abandoned by this same man in Tippah County at the death of their mother, he rode twenty miles to find them and bring them to his own

place. Several of the house servants at Heaven Trees appear
frequently in the novel. The account of Solomon, Dr. Clay's
valet, is based upon a Negro whose story was well known in
Panola County.[11] He claimed to be an African prince who care-
lessly came too close to an English slave ship and was enslaved.
The maid Scott Judy and the cook old Aunt Adeline are individu-
alized by brief biographies and anecdotes, while others are mentioned only by name. Although Dr. Clay has built a church at
Cistern Hill for his slaves, many of them attend the Fredonia
Church where they sit in the gallery. In the chapter entitled
"Romance," Young features an account of the Negro baptism
ceremonies at Jacob's Bayou and a midnight serenade by Negro
musicians at Heaven Trees. Both events are seen from the point
of view of the white family. The account of the baptism ceremonies serves to provoke a discussion of religion; while the serenade is seen as a part of the charm of life at Heaven Trees.
In both incidents Young emphasizes the beauty of Negro voices.

Scores of reviewers in newspapers and magazines wrote only
words of high praise for Young's character studies, his poetic
descriptions, and the charming atmosphere of *Heaven Trees*. Perhaps the only dissenting voice was that of John H. McGinnis
in the *Dallas News*.[12] McGinnis complained that Young, hitherto
a liberal, had joined the moonlight and magnolia tradition of
Thomas Nelson Page's Virginia romances and ignored the real
issues and violence of the antebellum period. In a letter to the
editor of the *Texas Outlook*, Young replied that McGinnis mis-
took the purpose of the book "which was to create a sort of
atmosphere that had in it a poetic glow and that without pretend-
ing to be realistic had a considerable salt of character drawn
in it and something of the loveliness of the Southern days and
nights."[13] What Young did not say and what the reviewers
missed was that despite the antebellum setting the characters
who appear in *Heaven Trees* are for the most part the persons
Young knew in the Panola County of his boyhood from 1881
to 1895, when he moved to Oxford. These people possessed
a vivid reality for him. As he wrote in *Heaven Trees*, "Their
virtues seem always of the heart, wise resolutions of the problem
of living. . . . I dare say every one there had grave faults;
and every one of them surely must have had his particular small
passions . . . ; but for the most part, at this distance, . . . they

seem figures of goodness and endearing life" (2). As much as anything else, the Southern tradition was for Young a matter of feeling, a feeling or attitude toward the land, toward one's fellowmen, and, especially, toward one's family.

Heaven Trees was Stark Young's first attempt to use the locale and the members of the McGehee family to express his vision of Southern life at its best. His book measured up to the standards of art that he had already expressed in his drama criticism; that is, in it he had embodied an idea and created something that had not existed before. That it was not realistic, that it ignored the violence of sectional conflict and the wrongs of slavery, did not matter to Young. What mattered was that he had used his own life in north Mississippi to catch the essence of the Southern tradition and to define those elements in it that made for the charm, the grace, the art of living.

The Torches Flare

The Torches Flare, Young's second novel,[14] represents a dramatic change in place, time, and tone from *Heaven Trees.* Whereas the characters of *Heaven Trees* had moved in the romantic, utopian, almost unreal atmosphere of the agrarian community of the old extinct town of Panola during the 1850s, the dramatis personae of *The Torches Flare* live in the harsh glare of contemporary metropolitan New York and urban Clearwater, Mississippi, Young's fictional name for Oxford. Although the place name Clearwater may have been suggested by Coldwater, a small town a few miles north of Como, it reflects the realistic tone of Young's book and contrasts sharply with the setting of *Heaven Trees.* Young's title phrase does not appear in the novel, but it implies the flickering intensity of art in the theatre that forms the background of the book. Yet despite the differences in approach, *Heaven Trees* and *The Torches Flare* leave no doubt that they are the work of the same author.

Young worked on *The Torches Flare* during the spring and summer of 1927. At that time he planned to call it "A Hundred Towers," but probably in the fall he changed to the present title. Perkins read the manuscript and suggested that Young rewrite several long passages of dialogue in the early chapters. He made the changes and Perkins approved them. By early

February 1928, the dust jacket was finished and Young was reading proof. The book was published in April.

For the jacket, which won the Atlantic Bookshelf prize for the best fiction jacket of the past year, the artist used a modern rendering of the Greek goddess Artemis, known for her beauty, maidenly modesty, and hunting skill but when tired of the chase fond of music and dancing. The artist has shown her running gracefully, her hair flowing in the wind, on her shoulder a quiver of arrows, and her left hand resting upon a hart's antlers, while her right seems to cast down behind her an apple. In Artemis, the twin sister of Apollo, patron of music and poetry, the designer may have wished to call attention to the Greek myths of Artemis and her punishment of Actaeon, who saw her unappareled, and Young's story about Lena Dandridge and Arthur Lane. The suggestiveness of the jacket design is increased by Young's allusions to these myths in his novel. For its second printing, Perkins printed on the back a sentence from a letter to Young from Julia Mood Peterkin, now remembered as the South Carolina author of *Black April* (1927), the Pulitzer prize winning *Scarlet Sister Mary* (1928), and *Roll, Jordan, Roll* (1933). Wrote Mrs. Peterkin: "The book is a poignant, heart-breaking thing . . . a beautiful piece of work."

Julia Peterkin and many other readers recognized the strongly personal aspect of *The Torches Flare.* The narrator, Henry Boardman, called Hal by most of his associates but Lafe by Eleanor (or "Lena") Dandridge, who thinks he resembles Lafayette, speaks for Stark Young. At the beginning of the novel, Hal, age thirty, teaches freshman English at Columbia. A Mississippian and former student at Clearwater College or University (Young uses both names), Clearwater, Mississippi, Hal has an ambition to become a playwright or novelist. Three years earlier, he had gone back to Mississippi to attend the funeral of his mother, and even more recently he has gone to Italy. For the present, in addition to teaching, he writes book reviews and occasionally articles on the theatre. His essay on Eleonora Duse prompted her to invite him to talk with her at her hotel. Hal's intellectual equipment resembles Stark Young's. Hal knows a great deal about the New York theatre, plays, painting, music, Greek literature, and Plato; and he has an extensive acquaintance with the inhabitants and restaurants of Greenwich Village. The ideas and opinions he voices are basically those of his creator.

Hal has known Lena Dandridge for many years; and at one time he had a romantic interest in her, but now they are just close friends. She grew up in Mississippi, was graduated from Clearwater College, and traveled abroad for a year. Her mother has been dead for twenty years. Her father, Dr. Abner Dandridge, has been a fine doctor. As the novel opens, Lena has come to New York for a change from the "vague round" of parties and "provincial monotonies" (6) in Clearwater. A beautiful young woman, she has successfully acted in several college dramatic productions. Hal and his friends, including Arthur Lane, endeavor to show her New York, their New York, the New York of the theatre, art museums, and Greenwich Village. Although she has had no professional acting experience, Lena's beauty and reading ability obtain for her the leading part in *The Rose Sleep,* a rather dull play by a mediocre but popular playwright. The play becomes a box-office success, and Lena becomes a minor celebrity overnight. Meanwhile, she has fallen in love with Arthur Lane. Analyzing the attraction between them, Hal thinks that "it was the man in him, not the poet, that Lena loved" (163). Although Lane understood little of her, he had the power of strong senses and strong impulses, a kind of natural mystery. He never mentions marriage, but Lena consents to the kind of irregular relationship possible in New York.

A proud Kentuckian, the same age as Hal, Arthur Lane is taking his doctor's degree at Columbia and writing poetry. His mother died when he was eight, and several years later his father remarried. Neither his father nor his stepmother had much affection for the boy. As he matured, he sought the praise and applause that had been denied him as a child, but what he most wanted was self-approval. He lacked confidence in his abilities, which, Hal thought, were considerable. Lane spent three years in the war, taught for five years in Georgia, and has been for two years at Columbia. After he falls in love with Lena, he demands that she sacrifice every relationship and ambition to him. He feels that her stage career is a threat to him.

In the spring, after *The Rose Sleep* has been playing since the week before Christmas, Hal and Arthur are offered positions on the faculty at Clearwater College; and when Hal returns

late in the summer from a vacation in Italy, he learns that Lena
has left the play and gone to Clearwater to be with her family
and Arthur. In Clearwater, Lena finds her relationship with Arthur difficult to sustain. Her father and her Aunt Bessie cannot
understand Arthur, and to satisfy him Lena finds she must lie
and deceive her family. What seemed acceptable amid the ano-
nymity of New York becomes morally wrong in Clearwater.
Increasingly she feels separated from her father. Moreover, Arthur is bored by her Aunt Bessie and Cousin Cornelia Backus,
who has come to live with the family. Other men begin to
seek out Lena. One of Hal's student friends, Eugene Oliver,
a sensitive young man who writes poetry, falls in love with
her.[15] Before leaving New York, Lena and Arthur agreed to
forego their sexual relationship while in Clearwater; but their
resolve breaks down one afternoon in the orchard. Oliver is
an unwilling and silent witness. Heartbroken, he leaves the college and soon after commits suicide. His death and the illness
and death of her father, as well as Arthur's irritability, increase
the tensions between the two lovers. Gradually she begins to
see what Hal has understood much earlier: that, despite Arthur's
physical attraction, he simply will not do. She is surprised when
he speaks of marriage. He explains that he could not say anything
earlier because he has been married, but now his wife has given
him a divorce. Lena realizes that their entire relationship has
been based upon his unspoken lie.

The plot moves rapidly to conclusion. Arthur angrily accuses
Hal of plotting to secure Lena for himself and leaves for Hot
Springs. He will stay on at Clearwater College in the fall. Lena
decides to continue her acting career in a new play by the author
of *The Rose Sleep;* and Hal will also return to New York, where
a publisher has promised to bring out his book, *The High Clouds,*
in the fall.

Young had created a realistic, contemporary plot that not
only enabled him to use settings that he knew intimately but
also served as logical vehicles for his ideas. The underlying
subject of the novel is the relationship of the life of the spirit
to society. This general theme finds expression in Young's depic-
tion of the artist in the metropolis and in the rural South. To
explore his subject, Young establishes several contrasts, the most
important of which involve a comparison between the artist

in New York and in Clearwater, between New Yorkers and Southerners, and between the academic and the creative life.

At the time he was writing *The Torches Flare,* Young was living in Greenwich Village on Grove Street, near its intersection with Bleeker. Nearby is Barrow Street, where Hal Boardman lives above the apartment occupied by Judith Boyle and Lena Dandridge; and to the south is Vandam Street where Catherine Sledge has her apartment. Just a few blocks away is Romany Marie's and close by is the home of Mrs. Courtlandt, a representative of old New York. Mrs. Norton's mother keeps her "boarding-house" on Elizabeth Street. Other scenes in the Village take place on MacDougal, Charles, Cornelia, Waverly, and Bank streets. Outside the Village, Young takes his characters to the Broadway theatres, the Metropolitan Museum of Art, Columbia University, the Casino at Central Park, Columbus Circle, and other New York landmarks. The specific place names help to establish the realistic base of the novel, and Young's extensive knowledge of New York artists, including playwrights, producers, actors, painters, poets, musicians, and designers, helps him to create a plausible milieu in which to ground his ideas. The New York of *The Torches Flare* is the New York of Stark Young; more precisely, it is the world of art.

The Clearwater of *The Torches Flare* is based upon Oxford, Mississippi, where Young was first a student and later a member of the English department faculty at the University of Mississippi. Friendship, the home of Dr. Dandridge, is a fictional, enlarged version of several houses built in Oxford during the 1840s according to similar plans. (One of these houses, Rowan Oak, which features a long avenue of cedars leading from bricked flowerbeds that were once parterres, William Faulkner was to purchase two years after Young's novel appeared.) Its builder, Alexander Backus, bears the name of Young's ancestor. In 1927 the grounds of these houses, like their fictional counterparts, for the most part had been diverted to other uses, but the lawns and vestiges of box hedges and parterres remained. Friendship house in Young's novel has been kept in good repair and stands in marked contrast to the Cedars, home of Major Proudfit Gordon Irby, a cousin of Dr. Dandridge. The Cedars had once been a rich plantation, but now only about thirty acres remain, "mortgaged to the hilt and rented out to a negro family on

shares" (252). The remainder of the land has long since been
sold, and Uncle Prout and his daughter Bogue are supported
by relatives. All that remains of the Cedars is "a square house
gray and weathered; around it there were a few cedar-trees,
but no lot, no garden, and no wall or fence; only a gateway
with posts remained" (255). Inside, what wallpaper remains
on the walls has faded to gray, and the Brussels carpets on
the floors are worn. Of the town of Clearwater, Young says
little beyond mentioning the railroad depot, the names of a
few streets, and the sound of the town clock. Of Clearwater
College, Young has more to say.

In writing about Clearwater College, Young had in mind
the University of Mississippi. While he was teaching at the University in 1904, an addition was completed to the Lyceum, the
oldest building on the campus, containing the administrative
offices of Chancellor Robert B. Fulton. The president of Clearwater assigns Hal Boardman a room in this addition. The artist
series concert takes place in the chapel, which had been built
in 1927 and named for Chancellor Fulton. Lena Dandridge
and Arthur Lane walk in the campus grove, and Eugene Oliver
joins a literary society instead of a fraternity. Even more closely
connected to the University of Mississippi, however, is Young's
characterization of the president of Clearwater.

In *The Torches Flare,* President Doyle is described as a "little
plump housekeeping sort of man." At Clearwater everything
depends upon his permission. "Intellectually he was as empty
as the trustees . . . whose conception of their relation to the
university was largely political, a matter of what professors
should be voted in and out and what departments given money."
When Hal Boardman arrives, President Doyle greets him with
a speech about loyalty and manhood, a set piece that "rolled
off his tongue like honey and gold." While listening to him,
one could not believe how nasty he could be with his political
enemies or that he could be maligned "by evil tongues, which
is how he described people who knew too much about his past."
His tenure was marked by unfair firings of faculty and "various
manoeuvres with funds and committees that honest gentlemen
like Doctor Dandridge thought shady and common" (222–23).

This harsh characterization reflects Young's attitude toward
Chancellor Andrew Kincannon, a former English teacher and

state superintendent of education. In June 1907, while Young was a member of the English department, the Board of Trustees appointed Kincannon chancellor and greatly broadened his authority to cover the hiring and firing of faculty members and control of the curriculum. Fear that he would be unable to teach effectively under Kincannon played a considerable part in Young's eagerness to resign his position. During the later part of Kincannon's term, he was accused of permitting politics to influence the selection of faculty and of graft in the financial affairs of the institution. President Doyle in Clearwater College is a fictional counterpart to Chancellor Kincannon, and Mississippi, especially Oxford, readers of *The Torches Flare* would have understood the resemblances.

For the most part, Young presents the realities of the two primary settings of the novel, New York and Clearwater, and leaves the reader to draw his own conclusions. Metropolitan New York, overcrowded, noisy, crammed with restaurants, speakeasies, and taxis, is unfriendly and anonymous; its air is like a "dirty soup." Yet it has its museums, art galleries, theatres, and symphonies. Agrarian Clearwater has its shady trees, lawns, flowers, and old mansions. More than anything else, it has quiet and peace, roots, and tradition. For Lena and Hal, going South means "going back to our own soil." Soon after he begins to teach in Clearwater, Hal stands at his window looking out at the stars and hearing the leaves moving in the trees: "Then a feeling came over me of what a man's own soil means to him and to be among his own people" (221). Yet a few months later, after having taken a long walk into the fields around the college and responding to the beauty of the evening star over the sad land, he finds himself lonely for what the country cannot give. He "felt a cry for the town. The city—and New York was the only city in America for me—seemed the only place to live" (263). For Hal and Lena, Clearwater may be regenerative of the spirit, but it is not the environment in which their art can flourish.

In Young's contrast between New Yorkers of the art world and Southerners, the metropolis makes a poor showing. The narrator comments unflatteringly upon many of the persons he knows in New York, persons whose lives are a tangled mess of human relationships. Many are second- or third-rate artists.

Among them is Judith Boyle. Her enthusiasm for painting and
her "chaotic honesty" (180) scarcely conceal her lack of pride
and taste. She has a series of passing affairs with the men she
meets while her wandering husband plans to found a love colony
as "the Redeemer" (132). May Coleman is a good example
of the inhabitants of Greenwich Village. Hal remarks that "her
grizzled hair stuck straight down from the edge of her tight
little hat. She had great silver earrings and a hot glamour of
black around her large open eyes. Her flabby cheeks and long
neck were powdered white as dough, her sagging mouth was
bright red" (25). Nearing the age of sixty, she still does the
Charleston. Clara Lorraine has a salon on Ninth Street, takes
drugs, was once married, and now has a young son named Sin-
bad. Seeing her at a party was like "tripping into a bank of
drunken orchids" (96). Hal reviews a book by Beulah Eisner,
"one of those novels that all my born instincts most detested"
(15). Hal remembers her cocking her eye at him "like a wild
fowl resorting to philosophy" (366). Later she writes a book
entitled *Words, Words;* in Hal's judgment she is "everything
that Lena made detestable" (369). Cleveland Towns, a piano
player and singer, drifts from bar to bar, entertaining for his
food. He could have jobs in acting, writing, and music; but
he is too often drunk. Almost on the same level with the Greenwich Villagers is that "breath of New York" (288), Mary Shannon, who gives an artist series concert at Clearwater College.
Hal describes her as lacking the warmth to make an artist of
any kind and having "no voice to speak of." Shannon's career,
notes Hal, is "with college bureaus of culture and under the
auspices of women's clubs" (286). To the friendly, gentle, and
charming people who wait to meet her at the reception after
the concert, she is rude, ungracious, and condescending.

   Young is equally severe on those associated with the commer-
cialized Broadway theatre represented by *The Rose Sleep.* The
producer, director, and actors are second rate. The best of them
is Herbert Anthony, who plays the father. Hal characterizes
him as an actor of the old school whose voice "seemed to come
from down between his knees, like a sepulchral bull" (70).
Like the inhabitants of Greenwich Village, most of the would-
be actors are lost souls, defeated in one way or another, and
typical of the hard life of New York. They will never make a

serious contribution to art, and their disorderly lives do not exemplify art in a healthy society. That Lena Dandridge could succeed in the play without any real dramatic training only underscores the low level of artistic achievement. Hal knows that Lena, with training and hard work, may become a good actress, but she will never be a Duse.

In Clearwater the people are not "very grand or famous" (287), but those of the Dandridge circle form a startling contrast to the New Yorkers. Lena's father, Dr. Abner Dandridge, long a widower, now in his seventies, had been a splendid physician, known for his skill in diagnosis and in treating children. In his dealings with others, he is thoughtful, tactful, and well mannered. After his death, Hal Boardman remembers him as "brave, and full of high spirits, pride, and recklessness" (318). Throughout his life, he had taken part in dangerous events—fires, floods, epidemics, and runaway horses. He never smoked, and like many of his generation in the 1920s, he strongly disapproved of women smoking. Without being a religious man, he held himself to a strict code of conduct that he followed "regardless of his own expense or what it cost other people" (319). He had no understanding of literature, art, or the theatre; but he enjoyed old style Southern oratory and reading aloud. Every young man of talent should aspire, he thought, voicing the Southern attitude of his generation, to become a judge or statesman. Young intended Dr. Dandridge to be a typical, if somewhat idealized, Southern country doctor and gentleman, resembling Young's own father.

The inhabitants of Friendship house include Dr. Dandridge's sister, Miss Bessie, a maiden lady who keeps house for him, and their cousin, Miss Cornelia Backus. Orphaned at ten by the deaths of her parents, Cousin Cornelia, like Stark Young's own aunts, has taught for fifty years, at times for "board and laundry" and at other times for only "board." In her old age, she has little choice but to live with her kin. As Hal knows, her presence in the family adds "the fragrance of old ways and gentle affections," but it also brings "contentions, hurt feelings, the wear and tear of age and temperaments" (276). Cousin Cornelia has one party dress which she calls her "thunder-and-lightning" (286) dress, takes an excessive interest in accounts of murders in the newspapers, and fusses with Miss Bessie over

inconsequential matters. Whatever their faults, however, Miss
Bessie and Cousin Cornelia are ladies and express the standards
of the Southern tradition.

Nine miles out of town lives Major Proudfit Gordon Irby
at the Cedars with his daughter Miss Bogue. Far more evident
than at the Dandridges, the household of Uncle Prout and
Cousin Bo reflects the decline of the area. The Irbys have maintained themselves only by selling and mortgaging their land
until now there is little left of their once large plantation, and
their house is going to ruin. Their relatives, including Dr. Dandridge, help to support them. Uncle Prout is a distinguished-
looking old man, a tall figure with white hair and a mustache
and imperial. Like many others in Clearwater, he thinks Lena's
career is in opera. Every year he is accustomed to spending
the summer in Asheville. His daughter, Cousin Bogue, is over
fifty—with flat breasts, dry skin, and gray gingham dress. Hal
finds her a depressing warning to Lena of the future of life in
the provinces. He thinks she wants to "forget the barren night-
mare of that gray husk of life" (258).

Wherever he goes, Hal finds unattractive persons. On the
train from Memphis to Clearwater, he meets Cousin Frank
Boone, a handsome but dull man and "so proud that he was
apt to take offense at anything." His pride had "walked him
out of one position after another" (207), given him because
people admired Hal's cousin, Boone's wife. Now he is selling
insurance: "if ever there was a man born for insurance that
man was Cousin Frank" (208). Even less attractive is Fatty Bar-
rell, the good-old-boy with the "football voice" (307), who
drinks at the fraternity house and arranges for the Senior Ball.
Clearwater seems to have few if any talented, worthwhile young
persons.

By contrasting life as Hal and Lena find it first in New York
and then in Clearwater, Young seeks to persuade his readers
to several conclusions. New York and the rootless inhabitants
of Greenwich Village are neither all good nor all bad. The
dirty city is full of people whose lives are marked by disorderly
personal relationships and lack of direction. But the city has
facilities that allow the full development of the individual, if
only he has the capacity to enjoy them, that is, to use them
rightly for the advancement of the human spirit. The South,

traditionally absorbed in politics and law, has left little room for the artist; but both the Southern land and its traditions, what Young would later call the life of the affections, have left a legacy that fosters the good life, even the life of art. Young was keenly aware of the South's shortcomings. He knew that the Abner Dandridges, and even the Uncle Prouts, were rapidly dying out, being replaced more and more by the Fatty Barrels and Frank Boones, whom William Faulkner would later call the Snopeses. But Young also believed that the Southern tradition still existed and that the best elements of it could be a resource to persons like Hal and Lena. In Miss Bessie's words, that part of the South will "never leave you" (378). Young never abandoned this position. To a much greater degree than New York, the South exemplified Young's conviction that "the health of a society . . . rests on the unity of its nature, and depends on the absence from it of hypocrisy, a confusion in desire and a culture that is false to it" (346). Writing in *The Pavilion* (1951), he could still affirm that he would never be a "full dweller" in New York. "I would live here and enjoy the protection it gives for gregariousness, solitude, or privacy, . . . and for the stimulation from many sources; but I should never find it the whole of life" (10). To that degree, Young would remain a Southerner in the North.

Hal Boardman, like his creator Stark Young, also faced a choice between the academic life and his art. At the beginning of the novel, both Hal and Arthur Lane are teaching English at Columbia University. As colleagues they have Professor Campbell, who covers his lack of creativity with ironical banter, and the arrogant Professor Levine, who has a good mind but is "revenging himself for something" (31). Hal realizes that Levine's personality is pathetic but knows also that it is ugly. Later, Hal and Arthur become successful teachers in Clearwater College under the dictator-like President Doyle. They receive offers of salary raises and, for Arthur, promotion in rank. At the close of the academic year, Arthur admits he has written no poetry, but he decides to accept his promotion and stay on in Clearwater. "If he stayed on in Clearwater," reflects Hal, "he [Arthur] would come to nothing, nothing lived, nothing written, only pride, languor, self-complacency, or defensive spleen" (304). He is not reacting against the particular circumstances of Clearwater College but against all academia, since he thinks there is little to choose among colleges. He leaves the profession with few regrets. Hal has reached the same decision Young made when he left Amherst College to strike out on his own in New York.

Young had touched lightly upon this same subject in the idyllic *Heaven Trees*. In *The Torches Flare*, however, he offered a realistic treatment of the limitations of the South upon the artist. Arthur Lane may have been intended to be more than merely an illustration of the incompatibility of the life in art with the routine of academia. In part at least, his example may illustrate Young's belief that the Southern environment was not conducive to creative work even though he had found the South a proper subject for fiction. The matter of the Southern legacy to the artist and society would continue to occupy his thinking and his writing. In his next novel he would take a slightly different approach.

River House

In the spring of 1928, while Scribner's was completing preparations for issuing *The Torches Flare*, Stark Young was hard at work on his third novel, *River House*.[16] A year later he wrote Ellen Glasgow that the book was finished and that Scribner's thought it the best he had written. Reading it immediately after its publication in September 1929, she found herself enveloped in its charm and thankful, as she said, "for this sad and true and beautiful story that is like home to me."[17] Julia Peterkin called it "real realism, full of wisdom, too, and pathos and beauty."[18] She added that Stark Young is "the writer, *par excellence*, of Southern people."

Young had reason to be pleased. The verdicts of his friends— and from almost all the reviewers for the national periodicals— were full of praise. Sherwood Anderson, Eugene O'Neill, Donald Davidson, Lawrence Gilman, Lyle Saxon, and Hershel Brickell gave the novel high marks for its portrayal of the problems facing the South, especially its younger generation.

Although Young had actually transformed his earlier play, *The Colonnade*, into a novel, he wished to dissociate the two works. Shortly after the publication of *River House*, he wrote

L. W. Payne, Jr., his friend and colleague at the University of
Texas, to request that in reviewing it he say nothing about its
connection with *The Colonnade.* Young considered the differences between the two works major. He felt that by making
the protagonist of the play an artist, who might be considered
to have a special place in society, he had limited its implications;
in the novel John Dandridge is an "average man," a businessman. The change in title was also significant. In the play the
colonnade is the central symbol and the Southern mansion is
called Flower House.[19] In the novel, River House, the mansion,
becomes the central symbol while the colonnade, now called
the pavilion, has a lesser role. Young retained the unity of action,
since the novel, like the play, takes place in two days and nights;
but he made the time of the novel contemporaneous with its
composition, that is, two years after the present time of *The
Torches Flare.* In addition, he added incidents and amplified the
characterizations and analyses of motivations. He made the character of John's wife, called Evelyn Oliver in the play but Evelyn
Chenowith in the novel, more sympathetic to John's position
in the quarrel between father and son. While *River House* retains
most of the basic outlines of the play and even much of the
same dialogue, Young's second treatment of the South's problems is distinctive enough to warrant consideration as a separate
work.

The plot of *River House,* like that of *The Colonnade,* chronicles
the history of the Dandridge family of Le Flore, Mississippi.[20]
Its progenitors are John Dandridge and his wife, both deceased
at the present time of the novel. Their children are Hugh (Alexander in the play), Edward, Rosa (Mary or Mollie in the play),
and Ellen. Except for Edward, they have lived in River House
for many years. At intervals the family has been increased by
two more or less permanent guests, Mr. Bahram Bobo, age
sixty-two, and Colonel Thomas Barksdale (Cousin Tom), of
comparable age. Seldom mentioned but not forgotten, Edward
(or Ned), after a youth spent in gambling and drinking and a
fight with a disreputable moneylender, was disinherited by his
father. The land and the family mansion have descended to
Hugh. At the unexpected death of John Dandridge, Edward
returned to River House and sought the land that he had originally been promised. Hugh, usually called the Major, refused;

but his wife, Obedience (or Bedie) took Edward's part. The dispute developed into an impasse; and when the Major accused his wife of being in love with his brother, the marriage dissolved. After denying any unfaithfulness and promising to return when he wants her, Bedie departed for Louisiana. At the time of her departure, their son, John Dandridge, was three years old.

As the novel opens, John Dandridge is twenty-five, and throughout his youth he has inferred from the almost absolute silence at River House about his mother that she is not to be loved or remembered. Like his grandfather, John has been educated at Princeton. Since graduation he has successfully worked in a St. Louis bank but has returned to help manage the plantation and live at home in Le Flore, Mississippi. He has been at River House only eight days when his father sends him to Louisiana to see his mother, now on her deathbed. In his brief visit with her, before the nurse sends John away for the evening, the mother has only time to ask about her husband and son and to give him a farewell kiss. The next morning John learns that his mother has died during the night. On his way back to River House, he stops in Memphis and suddenly marries Evelyn Chenowith.

In the opening chapter of the novel, the family is eagerly expecting the momentary arrival of the newly wed couple. At the same time, the Major waits impatiently for his lawyer, Judge Barr, to assure him of the legality of his claim to his brother's inheritance. Edward's son, Ned, has been writing letters about his father's portion, thus reopening the old dispute that has separated the Major from his wife. He had hoped to consult Judge Barr and dismiss the subject before John arrived, but Barr delays until the matter cannot be kept entirely from John's notice.

John's few moments with his dying mother have profoundly affected him. Her nurse told him that Mrs. Dandridge often spoke of River House, her husband, and her son as if they were her dearest memories. On the way back from Louisiana, John realizes that he has misjudged his mother. The vague reference shortly after his arrival to the legal matter increases his desire to know about the family's affairs. He asks his father to explain. Very reluctantly the Major unfolds the basis of young Ned's complaint and, necessarily, the cause of the separation between the Major and his wife. John quickly perceives that to grant Ned's right to the land would be to admit that the Major has acted wrongly toward his wife. But John sees no reason why Ned should suffer for his father's youthful indiscretions and holds, as his mother had done, that the legality of the matter is not an issue. Realizing that the Major's position has been false from the beginning, John takes his mother's side.

The Major, however, does not give up easily. Bluntly he asks Evelyn to use her physical charms to persuade John to abandon his opposition. At first she agrees and asks John to give the matter up; but a few moments later, as they embrace in the pavilion, she forgets what she had been asking and thinks only of their love. Mistakenly interpreting her question "Will you?" he promises to oppose his father no longer. The following evening Evelyn tells the Major that she will not help him; and a few minutes later, when John says that he cannot keep his promise, the lovers are reconciled to each other. If he should decide to resume his job in the St. Louis bank, she will go with him.

The plot reaches its climax soon afterward in a dramatic confrontation between the Major and his son. The Major charges that his wife has talked to John about their dispute, but he denies this accusation. John concludes that his father is still fighting his wife and excuses himself from further conversation. A short time later, Mr. Bobo learns that John has taken the train for St. Louis and that Evelyn will follow him.

Throughout *River House,* Young refers to Como, Sardis, Batesville, and Oxford, towns that he had used in his earlier novels, but identifies the site of Le Flore, where the Dandridges live, only by references to its being on the Tallahatchie River, two hours by train from Memphis, and populated by about two thousand persons. Greenwood, on the Tallahatchie River in Leflore County, more than any other town in the area, would have met these criteria in the 1920s. If Young had in mind Greenwood, his choice was probably governed by his desire to locate his novel in a town having a greater commercial development than could be found in the Oxford-Batesville-Como area.

Young heavily underscores the changes that have been taking place recently in Le Flore. So many of the generation of the "old Southern people" (243) have died that only a handful of the Dandridges' circle of friends remains. They have been replaced by people from the country back in the hills and a scattering of foreigners. These new people are for the most part storekeepers or workmen, and they have built little houses on the grounds of the older families. John Dandridge is sickened by what he sees has happened to Cassie Caswell, his former chum. In the past few years, Cassie has put on weight, his earlier shy manner has become loud and hard, and he talks like a booster and fundamentalist. John observes sadly that "Le Flore and time and the Rotarians had done their work too well" (243). Many of the old mansions, dating from antebellum days, have been torn down, and John foresees the day when even River House would be razed to make room for a pasture, crops, or subdivision lots. The town has become a noisy collection of garages, banks, churches, and stores; and the upsurge in construction promises even more buildings. There is great activity but no evidence that the rushing pace has improved the quality of living.

River House, the central place and symbol in the novel, is insulated from the town on all sides. A brick wall, clumps of bamboo, cedars, and liveoak and magnolias screen the house in front from the street, a main thoroughfare, less than a hundred feet away. To the west a formal garden surrounded by walls of liveoaks and outlined by four lead statues of the seasons is the Major's favorite part of the old place. On the southeast the Tallahatchie River, now a sluggish and quiet stream since the steamboats no longer use it for traffic, bounds River House. A walk along the river leads to the pavilion, called the Temple of Love, with its columns of white marble and dome of plastered brickwork. The pavilion had been the favorite spot of John's mother and his grandfather. Had not John treasured it, the Major would have torn it down long ago. River House seems remote, as if not a part of the town; and from it the Dandridges cannot see the world beyond.

The house itself is not the traditional square wooden building painted white with green shutters, having six columns along a porch and a small balcony above the front door. Instead, the architect has followed the style that the Spanish had developed in Louisiana. River House is oblong, built of brick, with eight columns, and, in place of a balcony, a second story porch. The parlor is on the second floor. Once very much used, it is now closed most of the time, its blue brocade curtains faded and its white walls marred by a crack between the black marble of the mantel and the stucco molding around the ceiling. Elsewhere the house is in better repair, but its age is beginning to show. River House, "one of the last of the old Southern thing" (167) is expressive of its inhabitants.

The Dandridges, "good Virginia Scotch-Irish" (40), have always been inclined to be clannish. They have a strong sense of family tradition. Their portraits, hung on the walls of the Dandridge sitting room, not always by the best painters, have dignity and style. Their choice in furnishings suggests that these items would interest them less than good taste in manners and conduct. Above all, they are land people who have, as John Dandridge observes, "lived in the land for generations, here in Mississippi and long before." Although they might not have made the point explicitly, "at the bottom of their hearts" they have a conviction that "in business you were not quite honest and honorable" (157). The Major believes that even the most honest man in business would not hesitate to lie for his own advantage. He thinks the profession of law has deteriorated in modern times. "Once they [lawyers] were statesmen and orators," he thinks, "now they play the game, just play the game" (11). Like most of his generation, he adheres to a strict code of sexual conduct and deplores the decline of social codes of behavior among his son's generation. He is convinced that "for most people society depends on a code and without a code they are lost" (83). Like River House itself, the Major retains unchanged the values that have governed his life. Whatever his lapses in judgment, to the extent that the Major (and his sisters) lives by a standard that is external to himself, his life has an order and a wholeness.

The Major's two sisters, Rosa and Ellen, implicitly defend the past, but their affection for John makes them more sympathetic than the Major toward the younger generation. Rosa and Ellen have taught school but now in their old age live with their brother at River House.[21] They do not approve of Evelyn's smoking, drinking, or choice of clothes; but they are ready to overlook these matters and receive her affectionately into the family for John's sake.[22] Their love and loyalty to their nephew at times border upon the absurd. They have, as Evelyn thinks,

"done their part in life and now so much of it was closed to
them" (123). Their world rarely extends beyond the grounds
of River House. They live mostly in the past. As Miss Rosa
says, "Everything I say . . . is about something that was over
long ago, we just don't know anything but the past to talk
about" (239). She thinks that all they have bequeathed to John
is a lot of "feelin's that can't do you any good, not in this
world these days" (70). Thus, Miss Rosa intuitively understands
the gulf between the two generations, a chasm she can only
bridge through her affection and loyalty to the family.

Many of these same qualities are observable in Mr. Bobo
and Cousin Tom Barksdale, the more or less permanent guests
at River House. Like the two sisters, the men feel the need
to express their individual personalities; yet they too live in
the past. John is dismayed by their lack of anything to do. Along
with his father, they have, as John thinks, for forty years sat
about, "looking after something now and then, reading a little,
mostly the newspapers, walking up to the square, eating, talking,
living" (244–45). For John Dandridge, coming to maturity in
the third decade of the twentieth century, the overwhelming
fact of life in River House is its orientation toward the past.
"In this old house where it was always reminiscence—No matter
what happened, no matter what was said, it reminded them of
some one or something in the past—never anything to come,
but always echoes, old music, the page was written all over—"
(176). The shortcomings that John Dandridge sees in River
House are the same shortcomings that Stark Young observed
in Como and even the university town of Oxford, Mississippi.
For Young they were the shortcomings of the South.

Although John recognizes the refusal of the older generation
at River House to adapt to the changing South, their absorption
in the past, and their lapse into a rigid formalism, neither he
nor his creator Stark Young is ready to dismiss the Southern
tradition as valueless in modern life. "It's quite bright now,"
says John, "to pick on the old Southern thing and show its
evils and all [as H. L. Mencken was doing in the 1920s]. Well,
I think it's more important just now to understand just what
it is. . . . I'd like to get a better line on this tradition" (164).
Only by dint of a struggle within himself does he reach his
final decision to leave his ancestral home and the agrarian life

it represents for a place in the St. Louis bank. He is already familiar with the alternative, for he has lived "outside," both in Princeton and St. Louis. While working in the bank, he has felt "boxed up in walls and streets" (156) and hated the dingy air of the city. He has left it because he thought River House has qualities that he could not find elsewhere.

As John examines the Southern tradition, represented by his own family, he finds a great deal to recommend it. To abandon River House would be to leave a great deal, for, as he says, "here there's some notion of the art of life, still, and it's going out of the world" (271). The thoughts of the old people at River House may rest upon the past, more specifically, upon a memory of the past; but John knows also that their actions are based upon principle. They stand for something; they have a point of view. River House belongs to his grandparents, to his parents, and to his aunts. "And from them to him and to each other," thinks John, "and from him to them, salvation passed; the salvation of our souls, passing from one into another, . . . because there is nowhere else to find it" (254–55). Whether he stays or leaves, they will always be on his heart.

So far as the dispute with his father is concerned, John understands that for the Major there can be no other position than the one he has taken for almost as long as John has lived. He sees himself as "his mother's agent" (285). His father has chosen to live by the letter of the law; John has preferred the humanity of his mother's side. His father has acted wrongly, has violated the tradition of the family, in both the matter of the land and his treatment of his wife. John would have felt even more strongly had he known about the Major's effort to use Evelyn's sexual charms to overcome his son's resistance. John's verdict upon the land would have applied with equal force in this matter: "It's the kind of thing we just don't do, that's all" (107).

The cleavage between him and his father becomes a factor in his decision to leave, but it is not the primary cause. John leaves because he concludes that each man must follow his own life, within his own generation. "The beliefs of his generation," thinks John, "and the direction his generation takes must struggle with deep-moving instincts and principles that are in him already." They change only very slowly, and as they change they must harmonize themselves "with the new belief and direction, which belong to this new generation of his that carries him along" (171). But in following one's generation, one must act upon his own terms.

He illustrates his point by reference to a Portuguese friend he knew in St. Louis. Manuel's family wanted him to be a diplomat. Although he worshipped his father and family, he left them and the family wealth because he wanted to be a painter. In leaving River House, John thinks he is not escaping life but only asking for it, "as Manuel asked for colors" (292).

John leaves to carve out his own niche in life, to be himself, to live in his own generation; but he takes with him the foundation of principle and humanity upon which the tradition is based. In some respects, his position is similar to that of Bayard Sartoris in William Faulkner's "An Odor of Verbena." Both young men recognize the weaknesses, even the failures, of their fathers to live within the tradition and both transcend it by turning its strengths into new directions. John may leave the South, but he takes part of it with him wherever he goes and will always return to it in his heart.

While many reviewers of *River House* understood the conflict of the generations as its principal theme, others emphasized Young's disenchantment with the South. In the retrospect of time, however, the novel is best seen as a continuation of Young's effort, begun in *The Colonnade* and *Heaven Trees* but expanded in *The Torches Flare,* to resolve his own conflict with the South. Implicitly, but at times also explicitly, in these works he is expressing the same kind of ambivalent feelings that later lay behind Quentin Compson's agonized cry at the conclusion of *Absalom, Absalom!, "I dont hate it!"* When Young thought of his family in Como and Oxford, especially his parents, his two Starks aunts, his McGehee uncles, aunts, and cousins, he could only think of their humanity, their devotion to the art of living well, and the "salvation" that had come to him through them. Yet he saw vividly their orientation toward the memory of the past and often their failure to meet the present. He saw too some of the depressing features of the small town in the South in the process of change from a rural community to a commercial, even industrialized town. Many of them were not greatly dissimilar from the small towns that Sinclair Lewis had portrayed in *Main Street.* They were filling up with the kind of people the McGehees and the Youngs had not known, people that Faulkner would later identify as Snopeses. At the same time Stark Young was grateful for what his Southern boyhood had given him. Thus, in writing *River House* he came to terms with Southern provincialism, though he by no means was writing his last word on either provincialism or the Southern tradition. *River House* must be considered an important work in the literature of the Southern renascence of the 1920s and 1930s.

Chapter Six

In Defense of the South

In 1928, not long before the crash of the Stock Market heralded the onset of the Great Depression that brought with it the bank holidays, the soup and bread lines in the big cities, and the New Deal, several writers and teachers at Vanderbilt University, led by Donald Davidson, John Crowe Ransom, and Allen Tate, were making an accounting of life in the South since the end of the Civil War more than sixty years earlier. Their first and most pressing question was simply: how has the South fared in the nation since 1865? The answers they gave to that question prompted a still more fundamental query: what kind of life provides the best conditions for the flowering of the human spirit?

Two years later the outcome of their discussions was embodied in *I'll Take My Stand: The South and the Agrarian Tradition, by Twelve Southerners.* The title was taken from the song "Dixie": "In Dixie land, I'll take my stand, to live and die in Dixie." Although the volume engendered a storm of acrimonious debate, it did not sell well; and its publishers, Harper and Brothers, soon ceased actively to promote it. What the twelve Southerners wrote in it, however, profoundly influenced the course of Southern literature, so much so that more than one historian has ranked it among the most significant books of the first half of the twentieth century.

The impulse that led to *I'll Take My Stand* had a precedent in Herbert Croly's splendid statement of American humanism in *The Promise of American Life* (1909). The thrust of Croly's book had been an attempt to restate American destiny in terms of the national purpose, defined in part by him as the "comfort, prosperity and the opportunity for self-improvement" of the individual American. Croly had emphatically warned his readers that the promise of American life could "never be redeemed by an indiscriminate individual scramble for wealth."[1] Out of his book came the essential premises of Theodore Roosevelt's Progressivism and the establishment in 1914 of the *New Republic* as a national journal dedicated to the promotion of these ideals. With the help of Stark Young, Walter Lippmann, Francis Hackett, and others of the editorial staff, Croly edited the *New Republic* until his death just a few months before *I'll Take My Stand* was published.

The immediate stimulus for *I'll Take My Stand*, however, may be found in the events of the mid-twenties. During these years the South, particularly Tennessee, suffered a barrage of caustic attacks from Northern critics, attacks that prompted the Vanderbilt Southerners to take a stand. From Baltimore, Henry L. Mencken, for example, castigated the South for its deficiencies and evils. His famous characterization of the South as the "Sahara of the Bozart"[2] depicted the region as a cultural wasteland. He complained bitterly that the South had no art museums, symphony orchestras, operahouses, theaters, or public monuments of note. The South, he asserted, had no historians, sociologists, philosophers, theologians, or scientists. Mencken found allies among Northern journalists. Throughout the 1920s, such newspapers as the *New York World* and such magazines as the *New Republic,* the *American Mercury,* the *Nation,* and *Current History* printed emotionally charged exposés of the Ku Klux Klan and Southern racism. In 1925, the Scopes "evolution" trial at Dayton, Tennessee, became the focal point of all that was evil in the South. Typical of the reporting of this trial were accounts written by Joseph Wood Krutch in the *Nation.* In one dispatch, Krutch, himself a native of Tennessee, charged that "in Tennessee bigotry is militant and sincere; intelligence is timid and hypocritical, and in that fact lies the explanation of the sorry role which she [Dayton, and, by extension, the South] is playing in contemporary history."[3]

In the eyes of the Vanderbilt professors and their students, the North was again trying to reconstruct the South through a systematic vilification of Southern life. Davidson, who thought he saw a stereotype of the South emerging in the Northern press, charged that the South was undergoing a character assassination. Southerners were being described as religious bigots, "Ku Kluxers," and lynchers. "We had hookworm," he wrote, "we had pellagra, we had share-croppers, we had poll taxes,

we had poor whites, we had fundamentalists." Turning to the
South's supposed deficiencies, Davidson noted that "we did not
have enough schools, colleges, Ph.D.'s, Deans of Education,
paved roads, symphony orchestras, public libraries, skyscrap-
ers—and not near enough cotton mills, steel mills, labor unions,
[and] modern plumbing." Instead, he wrote, the South had
"too many U.D.C.'s, D.A.R.'s, W.C.T.U.'s, too many Method-
ists and Baptists, too many one-horse farms, too many illiterates,
too many Old Colonels." The South's only relief from "our
dull rural life" arose from religious orgies and Negro lynchings.
He concluded, "We were a bad lot, a disgrace to the United
States—and the only possible salvation for us was through instruction from Northern sources."[4] Against this picture of the
South in the Northern press, the twelve Southerners who wrote
essays in *I'll Take My Stand* determined to protest.

Early in 1926 Tate, Ransom, and Davidson began to talk
about a volume dealing with the literary traditions of the Old
South, but soon they began to think more of a symposium in
defense of what they called their "joint Southernism"[5] against
Northern industrialism. During the academic year 1927–28 they
recruited several others to the cause. Frank Lawrence Owsley,
an influential Southern historian, brought not only a resentment
against Northern insults but also an outspoken enthusiasm for
farming. Andrew Lytle, novelist, editor, and teacher, expressed
bitterness over the disappearance of Southern folkways. John
Donald Wade, Longstreet's biographer and founder of the *Georgia Review,* strongly endorsed the ideas of the group. By the
time Tate left in the fall of 1928 to spend a year in France,
plans for the symposium had progressed further but were still
fluid. Davidson, Ransom, and Wade began to consider other
contributors.

Such persons as James H. Kirkland, Broadus Mitchell, Julia
Mood Peterkin, William E. Dodd, Gerald Johnson, and String-
fellow Barr were nominated, but only Johnson and Barr were
actually approached. Johnson had recently written a biography
of Andrew Jackson, and Barr, professor of history at the University of Virginia, was editor of the *Virginia Quarterly Review.* Both
men declined to participate. At intervals Davidson continued
to search and to discuss with Tate possible authors and subjects.
In the summer of 1929 Tate wrote Davidson that "*perhaps* Stark

Young, if he can be prevented from including anecdotes of his grandmother,"[6] might write on "the Southern Way of Life," but Tate really preferred Robert Penn Warren for the topic. At the same time Tate suggested John Gould Fletcher, the Arkansas poet and social critic, for an essay on education. Although Davidson had reservations about Fletcher because he was "too far away from the scene,"[7] eventually Fletcher and Stark Young became the only two "outsiders," that is, contributors not connected in some way with Vanderbilt.

About Young, Davidson was enthusiastic. He wrote Tate: "As for Stark Young, I think it would be extremely wise to have such a man as he is, if we can be sure he understands the full import of the affair and does not treat it simply as a literary or sentimental excursion." Davidson listed several reasons for the choice: "He [Young] knows the tone of Southern life at its best and writes extremely well; he comes from Mississippi originally, but has wandered widely enough not to be accused of narrow parochialism; we need at least one such eminent Southern writer, outside of our own circle, to strengthen our array. . . ."[8] Ransom also recognized Young's value to the project. Writing to Tate, Ransom said, "It is my feeling that we ought to get the benefit of his name if it doesn't sacrifice our principles—and of the beautiful English of his contribution."[9]

By the spring of 1930 most of the twelve contributors had been selected. In addition to Tate, Ransom, Davidson, Owsley, Lytle, Wade, Warren, Young, and Fletcher, Herman Clarence Nixon, an economic historian who had taught at Vanderbilt, and Lyle H. Lanier, assistant professor of psychology at Vanderbilt, had been committed. With the addition of Henry Blue Kline, a Vanderbilt student, admired by both Ransom and Davidson, the list of twelve authors of *I'll Take My Stand* was completed. Of the group, Stark Young was the only writer at that time possessing a national reputation.

After completing *River House*, Young had begun work on *The Street of the Islands*, a book of sketches and stories set mostly in Italy, Spain, and Mexico.[10] In March 1930 he made a brief visit to Bermuda, returning to New York to read proof on this volume, published in the fall of 1930. Waiting for him on his arrival, he found Davidson's request for a definite commitment to participate in *I'll Take My Stand.* Davidson enclosed a copy of a tentative table of contents and suggested that Young write something on Southern life under the heading of manners. Young hastily accepted the invitation to submit an essay and wrote a detailed commentary upon the topics named in the table of contents.

Later Young, as well as other contributors, had an opportunity to comment upon a statement of principles or manifesto that preceded the essays in the published book. Everyone was in substantial agreement that the agrarian way of life was the Southern way of living, that industrialism had had disastrous effects upon the human spirit, and that the good life was not a life spent in the competitive scramble for material goods. In addition, the contributors generally agreed that neither religion, nor the arts, nor the amenities of life could flourish under an industrial civilization. In their essays they discussed Southern history from 1865 to 1930, the industrialization of the North during these years, and developments in economics, religion, the arts, education, politics, race relations, and agriculture. Uniformly the contributors concluded that the promise of American life was not being fulfilled by industrialism in the South or, for that matter, in the North. The South, especially, they argued, must take its stand against the materialism to which industrial "progress" inevitably led its followers.

Long before Young was asked to take part in the symposium, however, he had taken a stand with the South. Wherever he had gone, from Mississippi, to Texas, to Amherst, and to New York, he had retained his strong Southern bias, a sense of being deeply rooted in the South, especially Mississippi. There, he realized, was the anchor of his life and the springs of his artistic vitality. Young's Southernness can be seen in his drama criticism, but it is more evident in *The Colonnade, Heaven Trees, The Torches Flare,* and *River House*—fiction in which he consistently voices a philosophical position consistent with some of the principles of the Southern Agrarians. In 1930 he welcomed an opportunity to make, outside of fiction, a forceful restatement of his views.

In late spring 1930 Young worked on his essay, despite interruptions caused by Croly's death on 17 May, the consequent upheavals at the *New Republic,* and his weekly contributions to the magazine. By 18 June, he had finished a draft and knew that his essay should probably be the last in the volume. He decided to call it "Not in Memoriam, but in Defense." Davidson and Young exchanged their manuscript drafts. Davidson made few suggestions, but Young advised Davidson to omit much of what he had said about the "Red Menace" of Communism. Young feared that if the book became too much of an anti-Communist political tract, it would lose its force as a positive statement of a philosophical approach to living. Later, he indicated that he was not entirely pleased with the final title, but he infinitely preferred "I'll Take My Stand" to "Tracts against Communism," the title favored earlier by Tate and Ransom. Early in October, Young read proof of his contribution, and a month later Harper's published the volume.

Despite the tendency of some essays in *I'll Take My Stand* to advocate a return to the South of 1860, Stark Young began his essay with an emphatic restatement of the substance of his three volumes of fiction. "If anything is clear," he wrote, "it is that we can never go back, and neither this essay nor any intelligent person that I know in the South desires a literal restoration of the old Southern life, even if that were possible. . . . But out of any epoch in civilization there may arise things worthwhile, that are the flowers of it. To abandon these, when another epoch arrives, is only stupid, so long as there is still in them the breath and flux of life."[11] He sought to identify in the Southern civilization that had perished with the Civil War those elements that might permanently enrich life not merely in the South but in every part of the country. "Though the South . . . is our subject," continued Young, "we must remember that we are concerned first with a quality itself, not as our own but as found anywhere; and that we defend certain qualities [of mind and spirit] not because they belong to the South, but because the South belongs to them" (336).

But when Young began to examine such matters as education, religion, and provincialism, he had difficulty specifying precisely those elements of the antebellum South that should be preserved. He noted that in the South the landed group at the top had given the culture its tone; he hoped that the South would return to the concept that university education, not professional or technical, is suited only to a small number of persons. Young valued education for its instruction in mores, decorum,

and values more than for the teaching of facts. In the matter
of religion, Young's approach was particularly vague. He called
for "a more modern religious thought for certain kinds of people" without specifying what the "modern religious thought"
would be. For others in the organized churches, he sought "a
return of whatever there was in the old that might lead to dignity, decent formality and tolerant social balance" (341).
Young's generalities doubtless reflect his own lack of strong
religious feeling, but they may also reflect the vagueness of
Tate's "Remarks on the Southern Religion" in a preceding essay.
In dealing with provincialism, however, Young was on much
firmer ground. He defended it as close to a "man's interest in
his own center" (343). Provincialism, he argued, "does not
at all imply living in the place on which you base your beliefs
and choices. It is a state of mind or persuasion. It is a source.
. . . You need not . . . live in the South, but you feel your
roots are there" (344). These comments are consonant with
the ideas he had already expressed in *The Torches Flare* and
River House.

From the assertion of Southern provincialism as a trait out
of the old South to be preserved in the new, Young turned
to the Southern family. Here again he was on familiar ground.
After observing that the Southern sense of family derived in
part from the traditions of those who settled the country, he
emphasized the relationship between the family and the land.
A Southerner, he argued, feels that his ancestors for generations back have loved him before he was born. One's position
stemmed from "the fact that your family had maintained a certain
quality of living and manners throughout a certain period of
time, and had a certain relation to the society of the country."
Southern culture, Young thought, did not imply any great learning so much as it was concerned "with a certain fineness of
feeling, an indefinable code for yourself and others, and a certain
continuity of outlook" (349).

At its finest, Southern culture produced an aristocratic tradition, and Young was at his best in defining its elements. "This
way of life meant mutuality of interests among more people,
an innate code of obligations, and a certain openness of life"
(350). In addition, it meant self-control. "You controlled yourself in order to make the society you lived in more decent,

affable, and civilized and yourself more amenable and attractive." These qualities, thought Young, constituted the core of the Southern tradition, and, as he looked at the past, he felt they were the criteria of good living. They helped to answer his basic question: "What is the end of living? What is the end of living that, regardless of all the progress, optimism, and noise, must be the answer to the civilization in the South?" (358). On that question, Young ended his essay and upon that question *I'll Take My Stand* also concluded.

As Young himself admitted, his essay was less a defense of the South than an effort to identify in the South the values that he thought should be continued out of the pre–Civil War past into the present. Most of the values he cited were those that stressed the continuity of family life and the responsibilities of the individual to his family and to society—the values of self-control, self-restraint, obedience to law, and respect for the order of society. The way to individual dignity lay through the individual's recognition of his obligations to measure his conduct by a code of behavior external to himself. Like most of the other contributors to the symposium, Young had his own brand of Agrarianism; and he was probably aware that among the participants there was by no means unanimous agreement upon either the term itself or the program it implied. Certainly Young had no social program to promote; he had no wish to advocate "dirt farming"; and he was not deeply concerned, as was Warren, with the plight of the Negroes. Though critical of industrialism, he did not seek its abolishment, because he recognized the inevitability of an industrial order in this country. Properly speaking, he was a humanist with a classical bias, and he was convinced that the hope for the South—and the North—lay not in a return to an agrarian past but in the revitalization of Southern cultural tradition.

I'll Take My Stand provoked a great deal of controversy from its critics both in the North and South. Ransom, Davidson, Sherwood Anderson, and others debated heatedly in print and on the platform with such opponents as Mencken, Barr, and W. S. Knickerbocker, editor of the *Sewanee Review*. Most of the other contributors made speeches and wrote articles in support of their cause. The volume was also to a degree responsible for a number of books, both fiction and nonfiction, dealing with the South's position in the nation. Except for expressing himself again in *So Red the Rose,* Young, however, took little or no active part in the discussions. Gradually, as the decade of the 1930s advanced, the rhetoric on both sides subsided. The movement never gained significant political support.

Agrarianism began as a statement of philosophical and moral principles by a group of literary men, and it retained its literary quality, which found its best expression in the poetry and fiction of such men as Young, Tate, Ransom, Davidson, and Warren. Like the Transcendentalism of the nineteenth century, which it closely resembles, Agrarianism voiced a deep feeling of protest against materialism. Its advocates called attention to the need for a reexamination of the principles and promise of American life and for a reexamination of the humanities of the South. Out of theirs and similar beliefs came the Southern Renaissance and, in addition to themselves, such writers as Faulkner, Tennessee Williams, Eudora Welty, Flannery O'Connor, and a host of lesser-known Southern writers.

Chapter Seven

So Red the Rose

Although ever since the days of James Fenimore Cooper historical fiction has appealed to American readers, throughout the 1930s it reached a high point in popularity. Doubtless the astonishing sales of Stark Young's *So Red the Rose* (1934) and the even greater popular success of Margaret Mitchell's *Gone with the Wind* (1936) helped to multiply the numbers of their followers. Southern Civil War stories multiplied by the scores until paperback volumes were available in almost every drugstore and grocery market in the country. Most of these novels belong to popular literature written without any purpose beyond the entertainment of the reader. Many of them, nevertheless, exhibit a respect for historical accuracy and a degree of literary skill. They lack the insight and the shaping hand of the literary artist.

A few first-rate authors, however, who used the form to voice their analysis of Southern history, have permanently enriched Southern literature. Among them, the literary historian would include, in addition to Young's *So Red the Rose,* James Boyd's *Marching On* (1927), Clifford Dowdey's *Bugles Blow No More* (1937), William Faulkner's *The Unvanquished* (1938), Caroline Gordon's *None Shall Look Back* (1937), Andrew Lytle's *The Long Night* (1936), T. S. Stribling's *The Forge* (1931), and Allen Tate's *The Fathers* (1938). Although not fitting the genre precisely, John Peale Bishop's *Many Thousands Gone* (1931) and Faulkner's *Absalom, Absalom!* (1936) should be included because of their treatment of the Civil War.

Although no single volume in this list towers above all others as the masterpiece of Southern Civil War fiction, the best of these novels would include those by Faulkner, Gordon, Lytle, Tate, and Young. Except for Faulkner, all of the writers had direct association with the agrarian movement, and all of them, including Faulkner, not only voiced the agrarian criticism of modern industrialism but also felt themselves to a degree aloof from the urban culture of the twentieth century. As a group they were committed to the humanistic values of classical civilization, they deplored the decline of the family in Southern culture, and they considered the Civil War the greatest single event in Southern history, the point from which historical developments should be measured. Of this fiction, Young's *So Red the Rose* is not only the most representative but also the most outspoken and persuasive. After reading it in manuscript, Allen Tate called it "a marvelous piece of work . . . the finest the South has ever had. . . . This is the first time the Old South has been really alive since it fell."[1]

Composition

Although Young had basically made his statement about the Southern tradition in *Heaven Trees, The Torches Flare, River House,* and the essay in *I'll Take My Stand,* several events tended to push him to write another novel of the South. Unsettling changes were taking place at the *New Republic* soon after Croly's death. Young felt the new leadership was departing from the founder's liberal progressivism and that he was being isolated and dismissed as *Southern,* now a bad word in the editorial conferences. The handling of the Scottsboro affair in 1933 shows clearly what was happening. Young urged the other editors to take a calm tone and view the trial in terms of its underlying issues and in historical perspective. He was soundly rebuffed, and the paper continued to publish sensational reports and strident editorials that Young characterized as its "ham method." In the attacks made upon the South, the trial of the Negroes, whom Young thought should be acquitted, somewhat resembled the earlier Scopes trial. As he saw his influence on the *New Republic*'s editorial policies diminishing, he felt once more impelled to defend his principles, that is, what he thought valuable in the Southern tradition. He decided to reaffirm and extend the position he had taken in his earlier fiction and the *I'll Take My Stand* essay. *So Red the Rose* would also be a personal vindication of his philosophy of life.

Even before the Scottsboro affair dramatized the breach between Stark Young and his editorial colleagues at the *New Republic,* he had begun to plan another novel. From the beginning he seems to have decided to move the locale of *So Red the Rose* from north Mississippi, the scene of his earlier fiction, to the vicinity of Natchez. He made this change, he said later, because he wished to depict an area where the houses were still standing, "good strong wooden houses—wood to the wood." He did not want it said that this novel was "mere romance."[2] Rather, he sought visible evidence of the life he described, not only houses but also photographs, clothes, and documents. Actually what Young did was to move the Panola County McGehees down to southern Mississippi to join the Woodville branch of the family headed by Judge Edward McGehee. To make this change, however, Young needed a great deal more information about the Woodville McGehees and the Natchez vicinity than he already possessed.

In the summer of 1932, at the suggestion of his friend William McKnight Bowman, Young made a trip through the Deep South, stopping at Como, Natchez, Woodville, and St. Francisville. In Natchez he admired a number of antebellum mansions, particularly their classic architecture, furnishings, paintings, and china and silver, "the richest things of their kind in America."[3] Near St. Francisville, he saw Rosedown, built in 1835 and furnished with treasures brought from many European capitals. Young was charmed by its magnificent trees, formal French parterres, garden sculptures, and enormous camellia bushes. Rosedown became the model for Young's Portobello, the fictional mansion of Malcolm and Agnes McGehee in *So Red the Rose*. At Woodville, he saw the three tall columns and part of the porch, all that remained of Bowling Green, Judge McGehee's twenty-eight room mansion, after Federal troops burned it during the Civil War. Young made it the model of the fictional Montrose, Hugh McGehee's home. Perhaps most important of all, Young met his distant cousin, Louise Florence Stewart, granddaughter of Judge McGehee, who would supply him with quantities of family documents and anecdotes. To her, Young would dedicate *So Red the Rose*.

In December 1932 Young again went to see Louise Stewart. She showed him paintings of Bowling Green and a long concert grand piano owned by one of Judge McGehee's daughters who persuaded a Federal officer to order the piano carried out of the house before it was burned. The piano and a few pieces of china "fished out" of the debris were all that remained. Young used both the piano and the china in his accounting of the burning of Montrose. Louise Stewart also had bundles of letters written in the 1820s and 1830s that somehow had been preserved. Young read them eagerly, absorbing the opinions, feelings, and day-to-day existence of his own "blood kin" before the Civil War. In the summer of 1933 he made a third journey to the Natchez-Woodville area to check details and get assistance from his cousin.

Young had actually begun to write his novel in January 1933, perhaps even earlier. By the fall of that year he had made good progress and thought he could finish his manuscript by Christmas, but the writing required more time than he expected. By May 1934, the bulk of it had gone to Scribner's. He had taken his title from a quatrain of Edward Fitzgerald's third edition of the *Rubaiyat of Omar Khayyam:*

> I sometimes think that never blows so red
> The rose as where some buried Caesar bled;
> That every hyacinth the garden wears
> Dropt to her lap from some once lovely head.[4]

Young was in Texas when Ellen Glasgow's review of *So Red the Rose* in the *New York Herald Tribune Books,* 22 July 1923, heralded its publication on the following day. She wrote: "It is . . . in my judgment the best and most completely realized novel of the Deep South in the Civil War that has yet been written."[5] Almost without exception reviewers praised Young's book. Within a month it had sold 400,000 copies and climbed to the top of the best-seller list, where it replaced Hervey Allen's *Anthony Adverse.* Eventually Margaret Mitchell's *Gone with the Wind* superseded *So Red the Rose,* but Young's novel continued to sell and has remained in print. In November 1935 Paramount Pictures released a motion picture version of *So Red the Rose* directed by King Vidor and starring Margaret Brooke Sullavan as Valette and Randolph Scott as Duncan Bedford. Despite alterations that left little remaining of the part of Sallie Bedford or the McGehees, Young was pleased with the adaptation. The picture was popular at the box-office and has had numerous showings on television.

Authenticity

Young intended his novel to be a commentary on a civilization rather than a history, but he also wanted authenticity. A large number of the incidents and characters in *So Red the Rose* had their origins in actuality. As he prepared to write, Young read, as he said, "thousands of pages on Sherman and Grant,"[6] as well as contemporary newspapers, commentaries on the Civil War, and such books as Lyle Saxon was writing about old Louisiana. Young's method in part may be illustrated by his rendering of the burning of Montrose. For it, he combined the piano and china episodes obtained from Louise Stewart with Sherman's account of the sacking of the Reverdy Johnson Hard Times Plantation on Lake St. Joseph, Louisiana. The destruction of Montrose thus becomes a "composite" but nevertheless "authentic" incident. At other times, he merely paraphrased newspaper accounts, an example being the passage dealing with the burning of Jacob Thompson's home (only a few hundred feet from Rowan Oak, later to be the home of William Faulkner) from the *Oxford Falcon* of 23 November 1865.

Often Young simply expanded historical facts. As the basis of the incidents involving Mrs. Wilson, mistress of Rosalie, he relied upon the letters of Elizabeth Dix Perrault, daughter of the mayor of Natchez during the War. Several passages are virtual quotations. Although Lyle Saxon had printed excerpts from them in his *Old Louisiana* (1929), Young worked from the original manuscripts. For his account of Lee's surrender at Appomattox, he used the eyewitness version of Colonel Charles Marshall, Lee's aide-de-camp. For the treatment of Sherman, the novelist borrowed heavily from the general's *Memoirs* (1875). In particular, he used Sherman's account of the death of his young son Willie and the confrontation with Mrs. Wilkinson. This material Young enlarged and rendered fictionally in the episode of Sherman's visit to the McGehees after the death of Edward McGehee at Shiloh. Sherman's account of Confederate sympathizers using a coffin and funeral wagon to send medical supplies out of Memphis to General Van Dorn at Holly Springs provides Mary Cherry with an anecdote. Young also followed closely Sherman's story of his assistance to Captain Boyd, formerly a professor in the Louisiana Seminary of Learning and Military Academy, of which Sherman had been superintendent. Edward McGehee had been a cadet in this academy. Elsewhere Young's use of Sherman's *Memoirs* amounts almost to quotation. For example, Hugh McGehee's memory of Sherman's remark that if the United States were crowded like Europe, it would be easier to replace the planter class than to reconstruct them is an accurate transcript of his words. Even closer to the source is Hugh's report of Sherman's characterization of the "young blood" sons of the planters. Since Young wished to make the general an important character, he was careful to remain faithful to Sherman's own statements.

To increase the atmosphere of historical authenticity pervading his novel, Young used wherever possible actual documents, persons, and places. Duncan Bedford's letter from Agnes McGehee to her daughter Lucy, Hugh McGehee's letter to Governor Sharkey, the wording of Elizabeth McGehee's diploma from the Worthington Female Seminary, and the quotations from Agnes Bedford's journal—all were historical realities before Young put them into *So Red the Rose.* Young's description of Edward and Lucy as children is an accurate account of a photograph of Howard and Stella McGehee, grandchildren of Judge Edward McGehee, used on the dust jacket of the novel. Equally historical are the names of the generals on both sides, the material dealing with the Civil War, newspaper stories, and the mansions at Natchez. Young later remarked that the historical accuracy of the novel had been praised by such historians as Douglas Southall Freeman, John W. Thomason, Allan Nevins, and Henry Steele Commager.[7]

Although Young maintained that only two of the important characters—Sarah Tait Bedford and Mary Cherry—were "portraits" of actual persons and that the remainder were composites and inventions, a large part of the cast had counterparts in real life. The former is a study of Young's Aunt Sallie Wheeler King McGehee (called "Sallie" and "My Dumplin' " in fiction and in reality); the latter Young had already introduced in *Heaven Trees.* In both instances, Young tried to show them "realistically," particularly avoiding in Sallie Bedford "a lot of 'Southern lady' slush that she herself would despise." He said that he showed her "slightly decaying in old age. . . . Yet it will require *intelligent* people to see how I am writing about a magnificent person and character. Others may think I created somebody rather *hard and difficult.*"⁸ Young modeled the fictional Aunt Rosa upon his own Aunt Rosa Alice King (in novel and life "Aunt Piggie"), though he wrote about her death in terms of his Aunt Frances Scott Starks. For many of the other characters, he drew heavily upon his memory of the McGehee "kinfolks" in Como and Woodville and even upon some of his friends in Oxford. Names of actual members of the McGehee family include Hugh, Micajah, Lucinda, Edward, Valette, Agnes, Miles, and Abner Francis. Although *Bedford* appears in Young's family, he probably selected it because of its English connotations. From the Bishop family in Oxford he took Mary Hartwell. He also mentions his father, Alfred Alexander Young, as a Confederate soldier of sixteen. Although many of these characters reflect Young's knowledge and opinions of his family, the line between fiction and fact is frequently difficult to draw in specific instances.

At least two of the Negro characters in *So Red the Rose* were taken from real life models. Billy McChidrick belonged to Hugh McGehee in Panola County. They were born about the same time, and Billy's mother had been Hugh's wet nurse. After the Civil War, Billy lived on with the McGehees and, when sober and not in jail, ran the cotton gin and grist mill. In *The Pavilion,* Young recalls spending many happy hours with Billy and confirms as fact most of what appears about him in the novel. Uncle Billy's parrot, which could imitate a seasick sailor, may, however, be fictional. Unlike Billy, who is both wild and irresponsible, William Veal is one of the most admirable characters in the novel. In actual life he belonged to the Stewarts. Young obtained a great deal of information about him from Louise Stewart, including the photograph of him that appears on the dust jacket of *So Red the Rose.*

Although *So Red the Rose* is a historical novel grounded in Civil War life and history, this aspect of the work can be overemphasized. Young, to be sure, sought to give his book the concreteness and air of reality that arise from adherence to historical authenticity. The use of such material helped to keep his novel from being dismissed as mere romantic entertainment; but Young had no desire to load his book with obvious data. Rather, he hoped that his use of family records, journals, letters, and garden books would be, as he said, "well hidden within the book."[9] He wanted to achieve something more than a fictional history. His primary object was "to create the life and the people that existed among and were partly derived from these conditions. I wanted that life thus created to be true to its original but at the same time essentially free of time and place."[10] Young, in fact, emphatically denied that he was really thinking of Mississippi or even Natchez. "The Mississippi end of all this," he said, "is partially incidental."[11] These remarks, as will be shown below in the discussion of the implications of *So Red the Rose,* are pertinent to any assessment of Young's achievement. For readers who consider the book a purely historical novel, Young may have failed to reach his primary objective, only one aspect of which was historical.

Events of the Novel

The plot of *So Red the Rose* cannot be viewed in terms of suspenseful action. It has no chief protagonist whose career the reader follows from an initial conflict, through complications, to final resolution. Although the Civil War exerts a powerful effect upon its characters, no single character, as in Tolstoy's *War and Peace,* combines both the public and private implications of the conflict. The war itself is kept in the background, and information about its battles is conveyed through letters, from newspaper accounts, and through the talk of returning soldiers. Young's focus is upon a large cast of characters, most of whom are associated with the McGehee and Bedford families, who stand for a society. Thus, the subject of *So Red the Rose* is civilization as it existed in the South and beyond the South as it exists in time. As Young said, "I am making it a comment on civilization and living questions. . . . I want it to be a large, rich and beautiful canvas."[12]

Although *So Red the Rose* may be interpreted in terms of a three-act play,[13] it may also be conveniently divided into three large movements—the prelude to war, the war, and its aftermath. The novel opens with an account of Hugh McGehee's birthday in November 1860. The opening scenes bring together the relatives of the McGehees at Montrose and the Bedfords from Portobello plantations. The families are connected because Hugh McGehee is the brother of Malcolm Bedford's first wife, while Hugh's second wife, Agnes Bedford McGehee, is the sister of Malcolm Bedford. As the multitude of guests and relatives assemble to celebrate Hugh's birthday, the reader has difficulty grasping these relationships. (In the second edition, at the suggestion of Maxwell Perkins, Young included a list of the principal characters.) Young intended some confusion. "The very essence of this sort of Southern society I write about is in the multiplied effect, the blur of company, then gradually the particular figures emerge."[14]

Gradually the particular figures do emerge. At Portobello live Malcolm and Sallie Bedford and their children: Duncan, a student at the University of Virginia; Mary Hartwell and Frances Scott; and Julia Valette Somerville, an adopted daughter. With them lives Middleton, the five-year-old child of Malcolm's dead sister. Sallie Bedford's sister, Rosa Tait, and their senile brother, Henry, also live with the family. Their slaves include Aunt Tildy and her husband Uncle Thornton, four maids named Celie, and Billy McChidrick. At Montrose live Hugh and Agnes McGehee with their children: Edward, absent at the Louisiana Military Academy, and Lucinda or Lucy. Their other two children, Annie Randolph and Belle Bowdoin, do not live at Montrose but return with their children for visits. William Veal is the family butler. Mary Cherry visits both plantations. This list includes neither the cousins, aunts, and uncles who form a large part of the more than fifty minor characters that appear in the novel nor the various generals and officers of both armies.

Although the confusion of characters in the opening scenes may make a reader impatient to get into the action, Young successfully conveys the sense of a large group of persons held together by common bonds of blood, friendship, attitudes, and traditions. He believed that the success of his work depended upon establishing the reality of the Bedford and McGehee families. He renders convincingly the speech qualities that individualize his characters. Throughout these chapters, the planters debate such matters as secession, the likelihood of Lincoln's election, and the possibility of war. At Christmas 1860, Edward and his father agree that the Union is best practically and politically. The McGehees do not believe in slavery but see no way of eliminating it. On one matter, they disagree. When Edward visits Jefferson Davis at Brierfield and returns full of admiration for the Southern leader, he finds that, upon learning of Davis's election, Hugh has walked the floor all night. Meanwhile, Aunt Rosa has died, and Lucy has fallen in love with Charlie Talliaferro, a wild, reckless but brave young man, a good example of the Southern planter type. The war begins in April 1861, and within a month, Duncan, Edward, and Charlie have joined the army.

The first movement of the novel reaches a climax in the conversation between Edward and his father just before Edward leaves Montrose. Young seeks to establish the sense of continuity in the McGehee family. Hugh recalls his father's grandfather who left Scotland after the death of the earl of Montrose and the outlawing of the MacGregors. Hugh wonders if this civil war had not broken his ancestor's heart. "You know how 'tis in our family," Hugh tells Edward. "It's something to know that you were loved before you were born." Hugh adds, in a passage central to the meaning of the novel: "Our ideas and instincts work upon our memory of these people who have lived before us. . . . It's not to our credit to think we began today, and it's not to our glory to think we end today. All through time we keep coming in to the shore like waves. . . . There's a certain fierceness in blood that can bind you up with a long community of life."[15] Hugh's words apply not only to family tradition but to the continuum of all human life.

In the second movement, Young deals with the uneasiness that pervades both families as they wait for news of their sons and loved ones and the Civil War comes ever closer to their cotton fields and homes. Information arrives slowly from newspaper dispatches and infrequent letters. In April 1862, when Agnes McGehee hears about the approaching battle of Shiloh, she has a premonition of Edward's death. With William Veal she reaches the edge of the battlefield before being turned back. Veal, however, finds Edward's body, and they bring it home for burial. Charlie Taliaferro, killed in the same engagement, is never found. Meanwhile, the Union army begins to live off the land, a practice that changes the character of the Civil War. Malcolm returns home from Vicksburg bitter with criticism of Pemberton and Jefferson Davis, who, Malcolm says, "had ruined the South" (248). He believes that if Vicksburg falls, the South is doomed. The Federals bombard and occupy Natchez. On 4

July 1863 Pemberton surrenders Vicksburg, and a few days later Malcolm dies. In his death the public and private events have coincided.

Young concentrates his locale at Natchez, where Mary Cherry reports on Grant at his headquarters in Rosalie. The Federals build stockades to hold large numbers of slaves who have fled from their former masters, often with whatever they could carry away. Some families in the city entertain Federal officers. In March 1864 Sherman stops at Natchez, frees a former teaching colleague from prison, and pays a call on the McGehees at Montrose. His visit is followed by the symbolic destruction of the planter society in the burning and looting of Montrose by Negro troops. At Portobello, many of the former slaves return, disillusioned by their taste of freedom. Having heard nothing from her Duncan, now a sharpshooter for Lee, Sallie plows her fields and helps a wounded Yankee soldier to recover and make his way back North. At the McGehees', Belle Bowdoin's baby is born on New Year's Eve, 1864, but dies the next day. Late in November 1865 Duncan arrives home, having spent months in prison. On the way, he has visited Washington College, of which Lee is president.

The final movement of the novel divides into two parts. One deals with the life to come in the South. Hugh McGehee had already encountered General Sherman, symbolic of a man divided between human affection and the callousness of modern machine warfare; in his wake comes Samuel Mack, symbolic of Northern industrialism and the impersonal forces of competition. At Portobello, Sallie Bedford likewise meets a representative of the new order. He is Sam Shaw, the poor white trash, now a businessman. The other aspect of the postwar era is represented by her son Duncan. In him that part of the South which Young wished to preserve has neither died nor been replaced.

As he rides out to see Valette, Duncan stops to talk with Negroes whose lives have been disrupted. Only the old remain because the young have gone elsewhere to look for work. Mammy Tildy tells him about the hardships his mother endured during the Civil War. Sustained by his admiration for Robert E. Lee, Duncan is ready to take up life again at Portobello; and when Amelie Balfour decides to marry Zachary McGehee, she easily persuades Valette and Duncan to join them in a double wedding. Although the novel may be said to conclude with these marriages, Young included a kind of epilogue or coda that is important in any estimate of the meaning of *So Red the Rose* and will be discussed below.

Underlying Ideas

Stark Young once remarked that *So Red the Rose* "sums up"[16] all of his fiction and carries the Southern theme as far as he could take it. In this last of his novels, he felt that he had said all he wished to say and all that he could say "with any fullness and creation."[17] His immediate subject had been not the Civil War nor Mississippi but the "whole Southern cultural idea."[18] The basic issues and characters of Young's novel, moreover, have their existence only incidentally during the years of the Civil War; and since Young is actually imposing his own point of view upon them, one could say that the real dates of the work should be not 1860–65 but 1932–34.

So Red the Rose is an intensely personal work of art. Stark Young's materials, as has been shown, came from his own family in Como and Woodville—mainly from the stories he heard from his father, uncles, and aunts who themselves lived through the Civil War in Mississippi. Young was chronologically closer to their generation and to the war than most of his contemporary novelists. He was, for example, born fourteen years before Caroline Gordon, sixteen before Faulkner, eighteen before Tate, and twenty-one before Lytle. Young's estimate of his material, moreover, arises partly from nostalgia but primarily from his double perspective of Como and New York, enhanced by his shaping imagination. His interpretation of the South gains intensity and seriousness of purpose from the fusion of his personal philosophy with his view of history. As a consequence, Young, perhaps better than his colleagues in fiction, is able to merge the public event with the private experience of his characters.

The cornerstone of Young's traditional society, as delineated in *So Red the Rose,* is the family as illustrated by the McGehees and the Bedfords. Family life at Montrose and Portobello emphasizes personal integrity, standards of conduct that lie outside of the individual, respect for the feelings of others, and the desire to enjoy (in the biblical sense of the word) life. They love the land and respect the order of nature; they are cool toward business competition and deprecate commercialism. They teach their children to subordinate their personal desires to the felicity of others, to know by "instinct" what should or should not be done, and to appreciate the continuity of life through the generations that came before them and will come after them. This complex of values, Young felt, was to be found among the planters of the agrarian South.

In Young's view of history, voiced by Hugh McGehee in *So Red the Rose,* the agrarian way of life had been under attack ever since the beginning of the Industrial Revolution in England. It had moved from England to America, where it dominated the North. In the South the planter civilization stood in the way of industrialism and had to be destroyed. The Civil War accomplished that destruction. Young recognized it as marking and accelerating the great shift in American society from a predominantly agrarian nation of small towns to a developing, urban, industrial country, a process that was continuing even as Young was writing his novel. The decisive battles in *So Red the Rose* were Shiloh and Vicksburg, which in turn were underscored by the deaths of Edward McGehee and Charlie Taliaferro and the looting and burning of the plantation houses.

Nowhere, however, is this point made more effectively and dramatically than in the scenes depicting Sherman's visit to the McGehees, Hugh's response to Samuel Mack, and the appearance of Sam Shaw. Standing, as he does, for the ruthless but effective military conquest by the North, Sherman is in person and as symbol the Enemy, a fact that Lucy McGehee recognizes at once. Agnes McGehee intuitively senses that Sherman is a complex person, tormented by his affection and admiration for the South, yet wholly determined to destroy it ruthlessly to gain his military objective, the preservation of the Union (and, symbolically, the triumph of the Industrial Revolution). Hugh and Agnes are profoundly touched by his visit; but in the conversation Hugh has with the general down by the gate, the planter realizes that Sherman is bent upon the "replacement" of the entire planter group. He is the instrument by which the Industrial Revolution will be completed. Appropriately, Young follows Sherman's visit immediately with the burning and looting of Montrose. The Civil War has spawned inhuman acts on both sides, as the hanging of the Yankee prisoners by a detachment of Confederates illustrates.

The "replacement" for the planter class appears in the person of Samuel Mack, to whom "society was actually a state of war" (386). Representative of the newcomers that have followed the Northern armies into the South, Mack illustrates what "competition without social principles" would become. Hugh foresees that unbridled competition would "lead to a legalistic attitude, law as the letter, the strategic game; and this meant the debasement of the social sense" (386). One cannot doubt that by 1934, when *So Red the Rose* was published, Young believed that what Hugh foresaw had become a reality. In this sense *So Red the Rose* is implicitly a judgment upon Northern industrialism and commercialism.

Sallie Bedford's encounter with Sam Shaw, the poor white, only underscores the same point. When he appears with a paper at her gate, she recognizes the same Old Sam Shaw that she had known in the past. Earlier he used to come "whining for something" at the "bottom of the back steps" (402). Now he comes with "his eyes full of sullen hate," presenting a bill for a saddle blanket. Duncan contemptuously tears it up, but his mother knows that Sam Shaw is only a sign of the times—"the bottom rail will be on top" (403). Sam Shaw's crowd will soon run the state. He is Stark Young's version of William Faulkner's Snopes clan.

The defeat of the South and the rise of the Sam Macks and Sam Shaws seem to presage a dismal future for the South; yet Stark Young did not concede total defeat for the values illustrated by the McGehees and Bedfords. The two marriages at the conclusion of the novel illustrate his affirmation of the continuity of life. Hugh McGehee, looking at both the young and the old, thinks, "In these people—they are my people—how much goodness there is!" (420). Their goodness derives from harmony, and Young declares that "it rested on a physical harmony and manner of life in which the nerves were not harassed; and it arose from the natural springs of feeling, where interest, pressure, and competition have not got in the way" (420). Young wished to retain this goodness from the past. As for the old way of life in the South, Young knew that "we can never go back" and that no intelligent person would wish to return to it.

So Red the Rose ends in a kind of epilogue or coda that reinforces Young's theme of the continuum of life. As Agnes McGehee sits with the young boy Middleton on an iron bench near Edward's grave, her mind travels back to that night three years earlier at Shiloh; and in her epiphany she resolves both sides of the conflict, not forgetting the past but knowing that life must move onward in the living. Young had not wanted his novel to conclude, as he said, upon some "booby optimism" or "sugar-coated rot."[19] He felt that *So Red the Rose* had a lasting optimism, and he defined its optimism as "that life rests in the individual heart and soul, along with an inclusion with the social general in which this soul and heart exists and finds its human expression."[20]

So Red the Rose is not a complete examination of Southern society. With the exception of Sam Shaw, for example, Young says little about the poor whites or piney woods people; and despite the prominence he gives to Negroes, he sees them from a white person's point of view. In evaluating the novel, however, one must remember that Young did not seek to write a fictionalized history of the South. What he sought was to identify those elements of Southern culture that could contribute to the good life for an individual, in other words, the permanent values. He identified them as the life of the affections and a respect for tradition within the family. At the same time, by implication, he deplored the competitiveness and pecuniary values of the urban, industrial culture that had emerged since the Civil War. He had also enriched Southern literature with his imaginative and artistic treatment of individuals who endured the trauma of the most dramatic crisis in American history.

Chapter Eight

A Life in the Arts

In 1935 Scribner's brought out Young's *Feliciana,* a book of Southern short stories, written from a point of view similar to that of *So Red the Rose.* The volume was well received by critics and achieved a respectable success in the marketplace. In 1937, Scribner's published *Southern Treasury of Life and Literature,* an anthology selected and edited by Young, designed as a textbook. The main thrust of his career, however, continued to be in the drama, but his work for the next few years would be strongly influenced by the external events of his life.

Young's pleasure in his accomplishments suddenly turned to bitterness over the death of his sister's son, Stark Young Robertson. A brilliant young man, almost an intellectual prodigy, Robertson had suffered since childhood from a variety of illnesses, and his mother had opposed Stark Young's desire to send the boy to Yale. Despite her objections, he enrolled in Yale. She had scarcely returned to Texas after visiting him during the Christmas holidays when he contracted pneumonia and died on 25 January 1936. Young blamed himself and never really recovered. Ironically, Young, who had praised the continuity of family life in *So Red the Rose,* now realized that Robertson had been the only hope for the continuity of his own immediate family.

The troubles at the *New Republic* continued to irritate Young, and he resented the shortening of his drama column. Toward the end of the decade, he saw with increasing clarity the decline in the quality of plays produced on Broadway. To be sure, there were some good plays, but not so many as earlier. There were revivals of established pieces, and Young wrote some excellent criticism about them, for example, George Bernard Shaw's *Candida;* Shakespeare's *Richard II, Hamlet, Twelfth Night, Othello, The Tempest,* and *Henry IV;* Anton Chekhov's *The Sea Gull;* Jean Anouilh's *Antigone;* and Sophocles' *Oedipus Rex.*

Among the new plays about which Young wrote brilliantly were Tennessee Williams's *The Glass Menagerie* and O'Neill's *The Iceman Cometh*. After the beginning of World War II, the theatre declined even more rapidly, and Young's despondency increased. During this period the single happy note in Young's life was his association with the Lunts, but it too terminated in disappointment and pain for him.

Chekhov and the Lunts

Under the management of the Theatre Guild, Young began a translation of *The Sea Gull* for a production by Alfred Lunt and Lynn Fontanne. Because Young did not know Russian, the translation required a great deal of tedious labor. His method was to make a literal translation with the aid of a Russian-English dictionary. Afterward, he compared his translation with seven other translations, making alterations as he thought necessary. Then he rendered his draft into a stage version admirably adapted for both the speech and physical movements of the actors. After road trials in Boston and Baltimore, the Lunts opened in *The Sea Gull* on 28 March 1938 in New York. By the time it closed on 30 April, the Lunts had given forty-one performances, and Broadway critics had pronounced it a distinguished revival. Throughout, Young had worked with the Lunts in the dramatist-actor relationship and established with them a personal friendship. Meanwhile, he had been greatly attracted to Lynn Fontanne.

Young revised his translation of *The Sea Gull* for publication by Scribner's the following year. In the preface to the published version, he discussed the problems of rendering Chekhov's lines for stage performance in English and included a series of "Notes for Actors," actually an extended commentary upon specific problems with the Chekhov text. Young's translation—he insisted that it not be called an "adaptation"—received excellent reviews and was later reprinted by Samuel French.

Encouraged by the success of *The Sea Gull*, Young took a leave of absence from the *New Republic* in January 1939, went to Texas to visit his sister, and began to translate Chekhov's *The Three Sisters* and *The Cherry Orchard*. At this time he employed a skilled Russian-English translator to prepare a literal

version of Chekhov's text. As he had done earlier with *The
Sea Gull*, he compared this translation with those of earlier trans-
lators and produced his own work emphasizing its "speakability"
for actors on stage. Eventually he also translated Chekhov's *Uncle
Vanya*, and in 1949 Random House brought out the four plays
in the Modern Library Series.

While in Texas, Young began to write *Belle Isle*, a romantic
musical comedy designed for the Lunts. The plot was based
upon Lyle Saxon's life of Jean Lafitte, the pirate. In Saxon's
work the climax of Lafitte's career took place in 1815, when
he had to decide whether to side with the British forces or
those of Andrew Jackson in defense of New Orleans. Lafitte's
choice brought him an offer of amnesty but ended his career
as a pirate. Young's play centers upon this moment of decision,
which is complicated by the pirate's love for a beautiful French
opera singer, a role intended for Lynn Fontanne. Alfred Lunt
was to play the pirate.

For Young, the venture, begun with enthusiasm and pleasure,
ended in unhappiness. He finished the manuscript in late summer or early fall, 1939. The Lunts seemed eager to act in it
and invited Young to meet them in Los Angeles to make certain
changes desired by Alfred. After touring with them for six
weeks, Young returned to New York expecting them to produce
the comedy in the fall of 1940. In April 1940, however, the
Lunts opened in Robert Sherwood's *There Shall Be No Night*,
which became a smash hit; in the autumn they took this play
on a road tour that lasted until December 1941. Young's disappointment was intense; he could not understand why the Lunts
had turned cold toward his play. In Texas he was shocked to
learn from a newspaper in May 1942 that the Lunts planned
to appear in S. N. Behrman's play, *The Pirate*. Suspecting that
there might be a similarity between his work and Behrman's,
Young privately printed *Belle Isle* under a new title *Artemise;*
and when he saw the Lunts in *The Pirate*, he was convinced
that they had betrayed him. Behrman claimed his work had
been inspired by Ludwig Fulda's *Der Seerauber*, but Young
thought he recognized many of his own themes, phrases, and
effects that he had discussed repeatedly with the Lunts. He did
not blame Behrman, but he felt certain that they came from

his own play by way of the Lunts. Young was especially unhappy at what he felt was Lynn Fontanne's desertion.

Painting

Despondent over the affair with the Lunts, the war, the *New Republic,* and the state of the theatre, Young turned to painting as an outlet for his creative energies. As an art form, painting was not exactly new to him. When a young man he had wanted to become a painter, an ambition strongly discouraged by his father as impractical; and at intervals throughout his life he had found relaxation in painting landscapes. In his poetry, plays, and fiction, he had displayed a remarkable ability to render into words his sensitivity to nature, particularly scenes featuring such flowers as camellias, peonies, and roses; and for years he had enjoyed friendships with such artists as Margaret Boroughs, Robert Edmond Jones, Maurice Sterne, and Pavel Tchelitchew. He sought help from Margaret Boroughs, who, with her husband, Wayman Adams, conducted an art school in Elizabethtown, New York.

By 1942, Young had begun to paint in oils. He rapidly developed a style of his own, specializing in flowers. A typical painting showed an arrangement of peonies or camellias on a table in the foreground, while in the background appeared an indistinct landscape, or a religious scene, or perhaps the horizon of a medieval town. Young gave literary or religious titles to his paintings. Often he included quotations from the Greek Anthology, Dante, Spenser, Leopardi, Racine, Keats, and Francis Thompson, to supplement such titles as *Garland of the Garland, Still Wouldst Thou Sing, Votive,* and *Ave Maria.* For a person who became a serious painter after he was sixty, Young achieved considerable success. In May 1943, under the auspices of the Friends of Greece, he enjoyed a "one-man" exhibition of seventeen paintings; and in November 1945 the Rehn Galleries sponsored another exhibit of twenty-five paintings. In both instances, critics reviewed Young's work very favorably, and he received invitations to exhibit at the major art academies and museums. Reproductions of three of his paintings were distributed on Christmas cards by the American Artists Group. Although

Young cannot be said to be a major artist in this field, he demonstrated in it a remarkable facility, and his paintings mitigated the depression that plagued him during this period.

Backward Glances

On 12 July 1947 Stark Young resigned from the *New Republic.* For twenty-five years he had been a member of its editorial board and throughout his career had published more than a thousand articles in it, including drama criticism, essays, sketches, and book reviews. Many of the same factors that prompted him to turn to painting also moved him to sever his connections with the magazine and, at the same time, with the Critics' Circle and *Theatre Arts* magazine. The decline in the quality of plays and drama productions, the trend of editorial policy at the *New Republic,* and Young's personal despondency lay behind his decision to retire. Doubtless the deaths of many of his best friends became another factor in his thinking. In a single year he mourned the passing of Doris Keane, Ellen Glasgow, Valette Sledge, Lyle Saxon, and Edward Sheldon.

At the urging of his friends, Young began to select the best of his essays on the drama for collection into a single volume. In 1948 Scribner's issued the work as *Immortal Shadows,* the title having been suggested by Young's sister.[1] Except for two of the reviews, which came from the *New York Times,* all of the selections had appeared first in the *New Republic.* Of the sixty-five essays, forty-eight were written before 1939. In his preface, Young explained the preponderance of material from the 1920s and 1930s on the grounds that in those decades there had been a remarkable movement in the theatre and that after the death of Herbert Croly the editorial policy of the *New Republic* "gave less and less authority and concern to the arts in general, so that with proper urging my articles got shorter and shorter." The state of affairs at the magazine finally reached a point where "there would be neither room nor encouragement offered me for any article of any length that in my opinion would have done credit either to the paper or myself."

From a vast wealth of material, Young selected carefully those pieces that would express the underlying premises of his drama criticism. Although he made no effort to assemble a history of the theatre between 1920 and 1947, the essays he chose not only illustrate the best productions of these years but also constitute a kind of theatrical history; and they provide incisive analyses of famous individual performances, outstanding productions of directors, and notable plays. From the 1920s he reprinted his commentaries on John Barrymore's Hamlet and Jane Cowl's Juliet, Eugene O'Neill's *The Great God Brown* and *Dynamo* and Pirandello's *Henry IV*, Gordon Craig's designs for *Macbeth*, Max Reinhardt's staging of *The Miracle*, and Robert Edmond Jones's decor for *The Birthday of the Infanta*. From his work during the 1930s Young chose essays on George Bernard Shaw's *Caesar and Cleopatra*, the production of Aristophanes' *Lysistrata*, Gertrude Stein's *Four Saints in Three Acts*, Chekhov's *The Sea Gull*, O'Neill's *Mourning Becomes Electra*, and Pauline Lord's acting in *The Mariners* and *Ethan Frome*. From the 1940s he reprinted his criticism of the Old Vic's *Oedipus Rex*, Tennessee Williams's *The Glass Menagerie*, O'Neill's *The Iceman Cometh*, Katharine Cornell's version of *Antigone*, and the acting of Canada Lee in *Native Son*. Young also selected his essays about the Moscow Art Theatre, the acting of Mei Lan-Fang, and the dancing of Martha Graham.

Young's announcement at the end of the preface to *Immortal Shadows* that "this volume represents the last writing I shall do on this subject of the theatre" prompted many to regret that he had not written a book, or at least an extended introduction summing up his final thoughts on the theatre, instead of merely reprinting his earlier essays. But the appearance of the collection gave reviewers an opportunity to evaluate Young's contribution. Almost all of them commented upon the uniqueness of his drama criticism and attempted to define his special qualities.[2] Philip Robinson's comment in the *Nation* may be taken as representative of Young's contemporaries' estimate of his work: "He [Young] focused," wrote Robinson, "on what was taking place on the stage not only a profound and cultivated mind but a specific theater sense, a developed eye and ear for the various arts of the theater, for which he had a deeply felt passion and about which he had acquired vast technical knowledge. He was able to see a dramatic production as a composite of elements of which the written play was only one, and could evaluate the specifically theatrical elements by the degree of their success in realizing the dramatic idea of the written play."[3] This judgment continues to stand.

Of all the accounts of Young's career, Eric Bentley, a leading American critic of the theatre, wrote in the *Kenyon Review* the most searching analysis, an article particularly valuable because Young himself responded to it.[4] After observing that Young could reject the dross and enjoy the gold in the theatre, Bentley called Young "a critic in the fullest sense—one who *judges* by *standards* that are not imposed from without but prompted and checked by his own first-rate sensibility." He was primarily concerned with defining his response to art in words that convey emotional feelings, yet "his ready emotionality is not divorced from his finer feeling or from his intellect." In this respect Young belongs with the New Criticism.

Despite Bentley's admiration for Young's sensitivity and aesthetic standards, Bentley pointed out what he felt were limitations in Young's criticism. He felt that Young exhibited a blanket preference for the Mediterranean over the Teutonic. This view may have sharpened his knowledge of Ibsen's shortcomings, but it blinded him to those of D'Annunzio. He excused in Pirandello what he blamed in Shaw. The same preference was responsible for his ignoring Strindberg, the expressionists, and Brecht, as well as his dislike of Odets and others in the social theatre of the 1930s. In reply Young denied any unqualified endorsement of D'Annunzio or blanket disapproval of Ibsen; regretted that he had nothing in *Immortal Shadows* about Strindberg, whom he liked; and had not thought to link Pirandello with Shaw. As for Odets, Young recalled that although he had earlier praised Odets's *Waiting for Lefty,* the playwright had later been greatly annoyed at Young's review of *Paradise Lost.*[5]

Bentley related his comments on Young's limitations to his "Southernness." Wrote Bentley: "Mr. Young is a Southerner and . . . an aristocrat. . . . He shares that blind animus against the whole world of liberalism which is the most limiting factor in, say, Robert Penn Warren's thinking." Bentley thought this fact explained Young's "failure to make more effective contact with the main stream of modern theatre—so largely liberal and libertarian in inspiration."[6] There is no doubt that Young was neither a political liberal nor a libertarian. He admitted to being a Southerner and conceded that Bentley may have been right about his attitude toward problems plays and the "drama of ideas," though he had never been conscious of such a bias. Young cited Euripides' *Hippolytus* and Molière's *Tartuffe* as problem plays that he admired and declared that he strongly resented tags of all kinds in the arts.

Although Young's Southern background may have influenced his criticism, it was certainly not the only factor. What Young did not say in his reply to Bentley was that in Young's view most of the problem or proletariat plays of the Depression era were not the best theatre art because of their excessive realism or naturalism, the topical nature of their theme, and their propaganda content. All too often they were poorly written, badly directed, and not well acted. Young's attitude toward them may have arisen more from his philosophy of art than from his Southernness. His artistic premises, which he had fully articulated in such works as *The Flower in Drama, Glamour, The Theater,* and *Theatre Practice,* also explain why he paid scant attention to such productions as the Ziegfeld Follies and musical comedies. In the theatre Young's preferences continued throughout his career to be conditioned by the developments he had experienced in the Provincetown Players, the Guild Theatre, and the Moscow Art Theatre. Bentley was correct when he exclaimed that Young "innocently" handed his "profound thoughts" to Broadway on a platter, "the platter being *The New Republic."* Whether he wrote from innocence or arrogance, Young's work met an enthusiastic reception from Edith Isaacs of *Theatre Arts* and Herbert Croly of the *New Republic.*

Instead of a final book on the theatre, Young had envisioned two volumes of autobiography: the first to cover his youth in Mississippi and the second to include reminiscences of his friendships with such artists as Eleonora Duse, Charlie Chaplin, Jacinto Benavente, Luigi Pirandello, Eugene O'Neill, Sherwood Anderson, Doris Keane, and, perhaps, the Lunts. Very likely, he would also have included Robert Edmond Jones, Maurice Sterne, Jacob Ben-Ami, John Gielgud, and Maxwell Perkins. Young may have thought that this second volume, which he never completed, would permit him to say whatever else he wished to write about the theatre. *The Pavilion,* subtitled *Of People and Times Remembered, of Stories and Places,* was published by Scribner's in September

1951. Earlier, parts of it had appeared in the *Virginia Quarterly Review*. He was pleased with the title, since he felt that it glanced at a passage from Psalms 31:20, "Thou shalt hide them in the secret of thy presence from the pride of man: thou shalt keep them secretly in a pavilion from the strife of tongues," suggesting the contents of the book.

Its nineteen chapters are remarkably consistent and consonant with the ideas he had expressed in volumes of drama criticism, novels, and essays. Beginning with his memory of a small waterfall created by the drop in the level of a culvert in Como, Young expanded this image, as was remarked earlier, into a symbol of the manner in which his Mississippi youth had presaged his life in the world beyond. Throughout the book Young sought to correlate his educational experiences, at home and at school, with his life as a mature writer and artist in New York; and in a wider application he endeavored to specify those contributions that the South could make to a person's preparation for right living wherever he chose to reside. For Young the answer continued to be what he had already written in *Heaven Trees, The Torches Flare, River House,* and *So Red the Rose*—the life of the affections and the humanistic tradition.

As might be expected, Young concentrates upon his early years at Como and his education in Oxford at the University of Mississippi. In retrospect he could deal candidly with their deficiencies. Como had all the problems of a rural small town, and the professors at the University of Mississippi were often not so learned nor the facilities so splendid as they would have been at other institutions; but he recognized them as the sources from which his life in the arts had arisen. In both Como and Oxford, stress had been placed upon good manners, tact, and attention to the graces and amenities of living. From his family he had learned to value relationships, to have pride in his family yet to cherish his own individuality, and to understand his role in the continuity of life from the past into the present and forward to the future. From the university experience Young dated his lifelong enjoyment of the Greek and Latin classics, literature, theatre, and Western philosophy. This humanistic education, more than anything else, had taught him to pursue the art of living. Moreover, in the light of Young's autobiography of his early years, his family training and university education, though not in the slightest degree designed to produce an artist, when blended with his individual talents and circumstances, fostered the life in the arts that he subsequently enjoyed.

End of a Career

For several years after the publication of *The Pavilion*, Young was engaged in various literary enterprises. He helped with new editions of *So Red the Rose* (edited by Donald Davidson), *The Flower in Drama, Glamour, The Theater,* and his translation of Machiavelli's *La Mandragola*. In 1955–56 his translations of Chekhov's *The Three Sisters, The Cherry Orchard,* and *Uncle Vanya* were performed at the Fourth Street Theatre and subsequently published by Random House with his translation of *The Sea Gull*. Young delivered lectures at Wellesley and Harvard and received the Distinguished Service Award from the South Eastern Theatre Conference.

In 1959, however, his literary activities were abruptly stopped by a stroke from which he only partially recovered. On 20 December 1962 his sister, Julia Robertson, died in Austin; on 6 January 1963 Stark Young died in New York. His friend William McKnight Bowman, who had taken care of him since the beginning of his illness, took the body back to Como for burial in the family plot at Friendship Cemetery, between the graves of his aunts, Frances and Sarah Starks, and near those of his mother and father. A short time later, several hundred of Stark Young's friends gathered at the Morosco Theatre in New York to join in a memorial tribute to him. Speakers included Zachary Scott, John Hall Wheelock, Harold Clurman, Martha Graham, Mildred Dunnock, Franchot Tone, Kim Stanley, and John Gielgud.

Young's Contribution

Long before 1950, when Stark Young was writing his autobiography, the kind of Southern education and Southern family life that he had experienced had largely disappeared from the South; and other writers, notably William Faulkner, had chronicled this disappearance with greater force and penetration than Young. The *New Republic* had undergone radical changes since

the days of Herbert Croly; and the New York theatre, especially
the part of it with which Young had been identified in his early
years as a critic, had also vastly changed. In such an atmosphere
Young was an anachronism, and perhaps, to a certain extent,
he had always been an anachronism. Although in the 1920s
he felt himself a part of a new "liberal" movement in the theatre,
writing for a liberal periodical, as the years passed he was more
and more often tagged as a "Southern" conservative, and his
defense of traditional values and his protest against the materialism of industrial, urban America were seen as perhaps commend-
able but assuredly futile.

Today Young's contribution as poet, playwright, director,
critic, essayist, novelist, translator, and painter belongs to cultural history. Of all the writers of the Southern literary Renaissance, he was the most versatile, yet only in theatre criticism
and the Southern Civil War novel did he make a significant
contribution to literature. In educational institutions men like
Harold Clurman and Eric Bentley recommend Young's criticism
to their students as examples of what criticism can become in
the hands of a superbly educated, sensitive, creative person who
knew the theatre as few persons have ever known it. America
has never had a critic quite like Stark Young, and until Broadway
has another renaissance such as it enjoyed early in the century,
the theatre may never see his equal. Young's fiction has also
been consigned to the literary historian, despite the fact that
So Red the Rose continues in print and remains probably the
finest novel dealing with the Civil War period written from
the Southern point of view. In fiction, as in criticism, Young
stood for something. In both he was consistently the advocate
of traditional values that derived from the classics and the art
of Western society. He belongs with all those writers who have
valued the life of the affections, the harmonious relationships
among them, and the importance of beauty and art in the good
life.

Notes and References

Chapter One

1. *The Pavilion: Of People and Times Remembered, of Stories and Places* (New York, 1951), 1; hereafter cited in the text.

Chapter Two

1. *The Blind Man at the Window and Other Poems* (New York, 1906); hereafter cited in the text.
2. Quoted in "Stark Young—An Appreciation," *Varsity Voice* 1 (19 October 1907):1.
3. *Guenevere: A Play in Five Acts* (New York, 1906).
4. Minutes of the Faculty of the University of Mississippi, 28 October 1907, University of Mississippi.
5. W. A. Philpott, Jr., "How the Curtain Club Was Born," *Alcalde* 5 (February 1917):285–86; see also "Curtain Club Makes Plans for the Year," *Texan,* 21 October 1911, 2.
6. Philpott, "Curtain Club," 287.
7. Howard Mumford Jones, "Dramatics under Difficulties," *Alcalde* 11 (February 1924):670.
8. George J. Hexter, "The Curtain Club," *Alcalde* 2 (April 1914):649.
9. Ibid.
10. "Music and the Poetic and Realistic Styles in Drama," *Drama* 1 (August 1911):135.
11. " 'The Drama' Accepts Seven Plays Written by Prof. Young," *Texan,* 11 May 1912, 2.
12. *Addio, Madretta and Other Plays* (Chicago, 1912); hereafter cited in the text. *Madretta* and *At the Shrine* were reprinted in *Three One-Act Plays: Madretta, At the Shrine, Addio* (Cincinnati, 1921). *At the Shrine* appeared first in *Theatre Arts Magazine* 3 (July 1919):196–203 and later was reprinted in *Golden Book* 16 (July 1932):77–82.
13. "Music," 128, 132.
14. Ibid., 133, 124, 125, 126.
15. See Young's review of Maeterlinck's *Pelléas and Mélisande, New Republic* 37 (26 December 1923):123.
16. *"The Queen of Sheba,"* *Theatre Arts Magazine* 6 (April 1922):152–64; hereafter cited in the text.

17. John Pilkington, ed., *Stark Young, A Life in the Arts: Letters, 1900–1962,* 2 vols. (Baton Rouge, 1975), 48, 45.

Chapter Three

1. Stark Young's name first appears on the masthead of the *New Republic* on 15 March 1922.

2. Warm personal friendships developed among the Crolys, Straights, Edith Isaacs, Elmhirsts, and Young. After a lengthy illness, during which he did not actively direct the magazine, Croly died in 1930. The Elmhirsts continued to make up the deficits of the *New Republic*—support that was very likely contingent upon the continuance of Young on the staff.

3. "Russia in Our Realism," *Vanity Fair* 18 (May 1922):55.

4. "Marketing Expressionism," *New Republic* 34 (4 April 1923):164. See also "Forward Equity," *New Republic* 34 (21 March 1923):100–101.

5. "The Moscow Art Theatre," *New Republic* 34 (28 February 1923):19. Young repeated and elaborated his criticism in "Many Gods," *North American Review* 217 (March 1923):343–52.

6. "Moscow Art Theatre," 20.

7. "The Prompt Book," *New Republic* 34 (2 May 1923):271.

8. "Bernhardt," *New Republic* 34 (11 April 1923):191. Although she had a limited range of ideas, she came closest to giving her tremendous gift "complete expression."

9. "Duse Now," *New Republic* 35 (20 June 1923):100–101.

10. "Miss Doris Keane," *New Republic* 29 (15 February 1922):340–41.

11. "The Prompt-Book," *New Republic* 30 (17 May 1922):343–44. See also "Giovanni Grasso," *Theatre Arts Magazine* 6 (January 1922):[1].

12. "After the Play," *New Republic* 29 (11 January 1922):183; cf. "After the Play," *New Republic* 25 (2 February 1921):291.

13. "Hamlet," *New Republic* 33 (6 December 1922):45–46.

14. For his estimate of Jones, see "Translations," *New Republic* 29 (22 February 1922):371–72; and "Hamlet," 45–46. For O'Neill, see "The Hairy Ape," *New Republic* 30 (22 March 1922):112–13; and "Eugene O'Neill," *New Republic* 32 (15 November 1922):307–8.

15. "The Failures," *New Republic* 37 (5 December 1923):46.

16. "Stark Young Talks of the Art of Directing and His Methods," *New York Herald Tribune,* 6 April 1924, sec. 7–8, p. 14.

17. Ibid.

18. "The Garland of Dionysos: 1923–1924," *North American Review* 219 (June 1924):876.

19. Ludwig Lewisohn, "The Failures," *Nation* 117 (12 December 1923):693; H. T. P., "The Failures," *Boston Evening Transcript,* 18 December 1923, 10.

20. Thornton Wilder to Stark Young, 8 January 1924, in Pilkington, *Stark Young,* 201n.

21. Lawrence Langner, *The Magic Curtain* (New York, 1951), 154.

22. In 1948 Stark Young dedicated *Immortal Shadows,* his volume of collected essays on the theatre, to the memory of Doris Keane in *Romance.* He wrote that "she was as it were all music and security of outline, like a swan on water, and something we long to believe can never cease." For Young's review of her performance in *The Czarina,* see "Miss Doris Keane," *New Republic* 29 (15 February 1922):340–41.

23. "Eugene O'Neill's 'Welded' Played," *Boston Herald,* 18 March 1924.

24. Gilbert W. Gabriel, "Linked Bitterness Long Drawn out in O'Neill's Newest Play," *New York World Telegram,* 18 March 1924, 20. See also Percy Hammond, "The Theaters," *New York Herald Tribune,* 18 March 1924, 16.

25. For Young's comments, see "The Garland of Dionysos," 875, and "Stark Young Talks of the Art of Directing," 14.

26. For Young's comments, see "Stark Young Talks of the Art of Directing," 14, and "Purely Technical," *New Republic* 38 (9 April 1924):184.

27. John Corbin, "The Play," *New York Times,* 17 April 1924, 15.

28. Young to Philip Moeller, 25 November 1923, in Pilkington, *Stark Young,* 200.

29. Young to Leonidas W. Payne, Jr., 2 May 1924, in ibid., 204.

30. Preface to *The Saint: A Play in Four Acts* (New York, 1925), 9.

31. Ibid., 117, 119, 121.

32. Alexander Woollcott, "Stark Young Submits 'The Saint,'" *New York World,* 12 October 1924, 16.

33. Young to Sherwood Anderson, 9 November 1924, in Pilkington, *Stark Young,* 217.

34. "'The Saint' Reveals Lofty Aim and Beauty," *New York Times,* 13 October 1924, 20.

35. Percy Hammond, "The Theaters," *New York Herald Tribune,* 13 October 1924, 10.

36. George Jean Nathan, "The Theatre," *American Mercury* 3 (December 1924):500–501.

37. Young to Charles Harbour, 14 November 1957, in Pilkington, *Stark Young,* 1393.

38. *The Colonnade* appeared in *Theatre Arts Monthly* 8 (August
1924):521–61; hereafter cited in the text.

39. "At the Play: An American Family Circle," *Manchester Weekly
Guardian,* 10 April 1925.

40. [Arthur Bingham Walkley], "The Colonnade," *Times* (London), 7 April 1925. Walkley discounted the plot as having "continuous
motion" but never arriving anywhere. For him the interest of the
work lay "in the langorous Southern air and the romantic summer
moon striking athwart the colonnade; it is in the negro music heard
monotonously rising and falling in the distance; it is in the dead quiet
and placid boredom of the old Southern home, with its faded furniture
and its faded family, its elderly gentlemen . . . ; its aged aunts who
are dissolved in mutual kindness. There is beauty in it all . . . but
it is the beauty of 'old, unhappy, far-off things.' " One struggles against
the play but in the end one is subdued by it.

Chapter Four

1. *The Flower in Drama: A Book of Papers on the Theatre* (New
York, 1923); hereafter cited in the text.

2. "Acting," *Theatre Arts Magazine* 6 (October 1922):279.

3. "The Flower in Drama," *New Republic* 30 (3 May 1922):283–
84.

4. Montrose J. Moses, "New Forms in the Theater," *Outlook*
133 (9 May 1923):853.

5. Ibid.

6. *The Three Fountains* (New York, 1924).

7. "J. W. C.," "Stark Young in Italy," *New York World,* 23
March 1924, 7e.

8. Mary Siegrist, "The Poet's Italian Baedeker," *New York Times
Book Review,* 11 May 1924, 13. See also Joseph T. Shipley, " 'The
Grandeur That Was,' " *Nation* 118 (30 April 1924):511; *Outlook* 137
(14 May 1924):70—a review of *The Three Fountains;* "Recent Books
in Brief Review," *Bookman* 59 (24 July 1924):609–10; "Stark Young
Essays," *New York Herald Tribune,* 18 May 1924, 25; and *Times Literary
Supplement,* 22 May 1924, 310. In Austin, Texas, however, Howard
Mumford Jones found that "Mr. Young's volume says nothing in par-
ticular, and says it pretty well. . . . Mr. Young is really half a century
behind time. He belongs to the age of James Russell Lowell" (*Dallas
Morning News,* 1 June 1924, pt. 3, p. 10).

9. *Glamour: Essays on the Art of the Theatre* (New York, 1925);
hereafter cited in the text.

10. John Mason Brown, "The Flower in Criticism," *Theatre Arts Monthly* 9 (June 1925):417. Brown's verdict on the entire volume was that "at his best, and he is at his best in almost all of *Glamour,* Mr. Young surpasses all contemporary critics when he writes of acting." *Glamour* is "the flower in American criticism."

11. See above, 38–39 and n. 5.

12. *Theatre Practice* (New York, 1926); hereafter cited in the text.

13. *The Theater* (New York, 1927); hereafter cited in the text.

14. Young to Payne, 13 January 1933, in Pilkington, *Stark Young,* 447.

Chapter Five

1. Young to Maxwell Perkins, 23 February 1926, in Pilkington, *Stark Young,* 249.

2. Donald Davidson, *Still Rebels, Still Yankees, and Other Essays* (Baton Rouge, 1972), 85.

3. *Heaven Trees* (New York, 1926); hereafter cited in the text.

4. Young to Perkins, 12 June [1923], in Pilkington, *Stark Young,* 191.

5. "Mad Money," *New Republic* 26 (19 July 1922):214.

6. Young's comments were made to the editor of the *Tait County* (Mississippi) *Democrat:* 20 May 1926, 2. To Ellen Glasgow, he wrote feelingly about the influence of his father's death and this visit to Mississippi; see Pilkington, *Stark Young,* 282.

7. Pilkington, *Stark Young,* 251.

8. *Tait County Democrat,* 20 May 1926, 2.

9. Many of the features of Stark Young's novels appear also in the fiction of William Faulkner. Both men often employed narrators who recalled their life experiences, and both wrote works that featured the repetition of family names over different generations and tangles of family relationships. Both were inclined to see the family as the basic unit of fiction, and each made his novels personal by using his own family as the basis of his fiction. Finally, both men exhibited a notable fondness for nature and an emotional attachment to the Southern land.

10. See Pilkington, *Stark Young,* 542, 1215. In 1935, while *So Red the Rose* was being made into a motion picture, Mary P. Poston, executive secretary of the Memphis chapter of the American Red Cross, in a letter to the *Memphis Commercial Appeal* recalled Mary Cherry and affirmed the truth of many of the anecdotes that Young uses in his novels.

11. John W. Kyle, "Reconstruction in Panola County," *Mississippi Historical Society* 13 (1913):17.

12. John H. McGinnis, "Old Themes Reappear in Stark Young's Novel of Ante-bellum Days," *Dallas Morning News,* 31 October 1925, sec. 3, p. 7. See also Pilkington, *Stark Young,* 255.

13. Quoted in "Young Known in Texas," *Texas Outlook* 11 (January 1927):46.

14. *The Torches Flare* (New York, 1928); hereafter cited in the text.

15. Hubert McAlexander, Jr., has suggested that the character of Eugene Oliver strongly resembles William Faulkner. McAlexander cites physical likenesses and similarities between Oliver's genealogy and that of Faulkner but notes that they do not extend to Oliver's role in the novel. See Hubert McAlexander, Jr., "William Faulkner— The Young Poet in Stark Young's *The Torches Flare,*" *American Literature* 43 (January 1972):647–49.

16. *River House* (New York, 1929); hereafter cited in the text.

17. Dust jacket of Young's *The Street of the Islands* (New York, 1930); see also Pilkington, *Stark Young,* 293.

18. Her comment was quoted in Scribner's advertisement for *River House* in the *New York Times Book Review,* 8 December 1929, 30; see also Pilkington, *Stark Young,* 295.

19. Le Flore, Young's name for the town in which River House is located, may have been chosen from a desire to retain the implications of the "flower" association in *The Colonnade.* In actuality, the county of Le Flore—and a small town of that name—is named for Greenwood LeFlore, a famous Choctaw chief.

20. Young connects the Dandridge family of *River House* with the Dandridges of *The Torches Flare.* Miss Rosa speaks of Alexander Dandridge and his sister, Elizabeth (Bessie), whom they have not seen since John was a baby. In *The Torches Flare,* Alexander is named Abner. Miss Rosa also mentions Cousin Al's (Cousin Ab's) daughter, Lena, as now grown and a New York actress.

21. Apparently, Ellen is the older of the two sisters, having been "born just before the surrender" (298). Rosa's age is not given. In *The Colonnade* the Major is seventy, but in *River House* his age is given as sixty. Young may have made him younger in the novel to leave no doubt about his active participation in the affairs of the plantation.

22. At twenty-four Evelyn is a thoroughly modern woman of the 1920s. Her father had been a lawyer and federal judge and was now a retired congressman. His second wife had been "some sort of political widow" (77) in Washington, "a tall, heavy woman with an enormous bust," large mouth, and a "coarse, foolish face" (78). Evelyn had no communication with either of them: listening to her windbag father made her sick and she disliked her stepmother. At

her marriage Evelyn has five trunks of clothes but little else. She cares nothing for books or prints, does not even know how long the Civil War lasted, and cannot tell the difference between Beaune and claret. She and John had been sexually intimate two years before they discovered their love for each other. Although her life in Memphis has been one of dissipation, her "heart was clear and good" (123) and she is intelligent. Her character and life-style stand in startling contrast to those of Rosa and Ellen.

Chapter Six

1. Herbert Croly, *The Promise of American Life* (New York: Macmillan Co., 1909), 24.
2. H[enry] L[ouis] Mencken, *Prejudices: Second Series* (New York, 1920), 136.
3. Joseph Wood Krutch, "Tennessee: Where Cowards Rule," *Nation* 121 (15 July 1925):89.
4. Donald Davidson, "Counterattack, 1930–1940; The South against Leviathan," in *Southern Writers in the Modern World* (Athens, Ga., 1958), 35–36.
5. Ransom's term in a letter to Allen Tate, 25 June [1927?]; cf. Virginia Jean Rock, "The Making and Meaning of *I'll Take My Stand*" (Ph.D. diss., University of Minnesota, 1961), 224–25.
6. John Tyree Fain and Thomas Daniel Young, eds., *The Literary Correspondence of Donald Davidson and Allen Tate* (Athens, Ga., 1974), 232.
7. Ibid., 236.
8. Davidson to Tate, 26 October 1929, in ibid.
9. Ransom to Tate, 22 February 1930, quoted in Rock, *"I'll Take My Stand,"* 238.
10. *The Street of the Islands* (New York, 1930).
11. "Not in Memoriam, but in Defense," in *I'll Take My Stand: The South and the Agrarian Tradition, by Twelve Southerners* (New York, 1930), 328; hereafter cited in the text.

Chapter Seven

1. Pilkington, *Stark Young*, 527.
2. Ibid., 1216.
3. Ibid., 413.
4. The title applies only loosely to the content of the novel. The verses suggest that the blood spilled in civil strife will enhance the beauty of the rose. The garden image also underscores the agrarian

theme and the beauty of the Southern land. Throughout the novel, Young uses the rose image, the most pointed reference being Edward's departure for the war. As he leaves, Lucy, startled by her father's footsteps in the garden, cuts off an entire branch of the rose she is pruning. For a discussion of the rose symbolism in the novel, see G. Frank Burns, "The Influence of Southern Agrarianism in the Novels of Stark Young" (Ph.D. diss., Vanderbilt University, 1973), 175–78.

5. Ellen Glasgow, "A Memorable Novel of the Old Deep South," *New York Herald Tribune Books,* 22 July 1934, 1. In her review she changed slightly the comment she had made for the dust jacket: "There has never been a novel of the South in the Civil War that can compare with it." Young was disappointed at the change which he attributed to her unwillingness to accord a rival author the highest praise. See Pilkington, *Stark Young,* 532, 1168.

6. Pilkington, *Stark Young,* 535.

7. Ibid., 1209.

8. Ibid., 518.

9. Ibid., 535.

10. Ibid.

11. Ibid., 1209.

12. Ibid., 449.

13. Cf. Burns, 138–40.

14. Pilkington, *Stark Young,* 538.

15. *So Red the Rose* (New York, 1934), 150–51; hereafter cited in the text.

16. Pilkington, *Stark Young,* 1209.

17. Ibid., 714.

18. Ibid., 1209.

19. Ibid., 1218.

20. Ibid.

Chapter Eight

1. *Immortal Shadows* (New York, 1948).

2. Among many reviews, see especially "Farewell Appearance," *Time,* 13 December 1948, 69; Harold Hobson, "Theater Critic upon Theater Critic," *Christian Science Monitor,* 2 March 1949, 2; Philip Robinson, "Theater Critic," *Nation* 168 (5 March 1949):666.

3. Robinson, "Theatre Critic," 666.

4. Eric Bentley, "An American Theatre Critic! (or the China in the Bull Shop)," *Kenyon Review* 12 (Winter 1950):138–47; Pilkington, *Stark Young,* 1129–35. Bentley's essay was reprinted in his *In Search of Theater* (New York, 1975), 266–77.

5. Young praised Odets's *Till the Day I Die* and *Waiting for Lefty* in "Lefty and Nazi," *New Republic* 82 (10 April 1935):247; he had reviewed Odets's *Paradise Lost* in "Quite Worth Your Thought," *New Republic* 85 (25 December 1935):202; for a discussion of Odets's reaction and Young's defense, see Pilkington, *Stark Young,* 651–53, 655–59.

6. Thirty years later Bentley again voiced his opinion that Young's drama criticism was biased by his Southernness. In a lecture given at the Stark Young Centennial Celebration held at the University of Mississippi, 11 October 1981, Bentley declared that every critic has certain biases, and "Young was no exception." Yet Bentley hastened to add, "Still, the effort was to see each work of art in artistic terms. In intention if not always in practice, Stark Young gave every work a fair inning, a fair chance to be a work of art." Bentley's lecture has been published in *Theatre* (Yale) 14 (Winter 1982):47–53.

Selected Bibliography

For a bibliography of Stark Young's writings to 1953, the reader is referred to Bedford Thurman's "Stark Young: A Bibliography of His Writings with a Selective Index to His Criticism of the Arts" (Ph.D. diss., Cornell University, 1954). The present list is limited to the more significant works; it does not include Young's articles in periodicals and newspapers; for these items see Thurman's bibliography.

PRIMARY SOURCES

1. Theatre

The Flower in Drama. New York: Charles Scribner's Sons, 1923.

The Flower in Drama & Glamour. Rev. ed. New York: Charles Scribner's Sons, 1955.

Glamour: Essays on the Art of the Theatre. New York: Charles Scribner's Sons, 1925.

Immortal Shadows: A Book of Dramatic Criticism. New York: Charles Scribner's Sons, 1948.

The Theater. New York: George H. Doran Co., 1927.

The Theater. New York: Hill & Wang, 1958.

Theatre Practice. New York: Charles Scribner's Sons, 1926.

2. Fiction

Heaven Trees. New York: Charles Scribner's Sons, 1926.

River House. New York: Charles Scribner's Sons, 1929.

So Red the Rose. New York: Charles Scribner's Sons, 1934.

So Red the Rose. Introduction by Donald Davidson. New York: Charles Scribner's Sons, 1953.

The Street of the Islands. New York: Charles Scribner's Sons, 1930.

The Torches Flare. New York: Charles Scribner's Sons, 1928.

3. Plays

Addio, Madretta and Other Plays. Chicago: Charles H. Sergel & Co., 1912.

Artemise. Austin, Tex.: Privately printed, 1942.

The Colonnade. New York: Theatre Arts, 1924.

Guenevere. New York: Grafton Press, 1906.

The Queen of Sheba. Theatre Arts, 1922.
The Saint. New York: Boni & Liveright, 1925.
Sweet Times and The Blue Policeman. New York: Henry Holt & Co., 1925.
Three One-Act Plays: Madretta, At the Shrine, Addio. Cincinnati: Stewart Kidd Co., 1921.
The Twilight Saint. New York: Samuel French, 1925.

4. Miscellaneous (sketches, essays, travel)
Encaustics. New York: New Republic, 1926.
Feliciana. New York: Charles Scribner's Sons, 1935.
"Not in Memoriam, But in Defense." In *I'll Take My Stand: The South and the Agrarian Tradition, by Twelve Southerners.* New York: Harper & Brothers, 1930.
The Three Fountains. New York: Charles Scribner's Sons, 1924.

5. Translations
Chekhov, Anton. *Best Plays of Chekhov: The Sea Gull; Uncle Vanya; The Three Sisters; The Cherry Orchard.* Translated by Stark Young. New York: Modern Library, 1956.
———*The Sea Gull.* Translated by Stark Young. New York: Charles Scribner's Sons, 1939.
Machiavelli, Niccolo. *Mandragola.* Translated by Stark Young. New York: Macaulay Co., 1927.

6. Autobiography
The Pavilion. New York: Charles Scribner's Sons, 1951.

7. Poetry
The Blind Man at the Window and Other Poems. New York: Grafton Press, 1906.

8. Correspondence
Stark Young: A Life in the Arts: Letters, 1900–1962. Edited by John Pilkington. 2 vols. Baton Rouge: Louisiana State University Press, 1975.

9. Edited works
The English Humorists of the Eighteenth Century by W. M. Thackeray. Boston: Ginn & Co., 1911.
Selected Poems of Sidney Lanier. New York: Charles Scribner's Sons, 1947.
Southern Treasury of Life and Literature. New York: Charles Scribner's Sons, 1937.

SECONDARY SOURCES

Anderson, Elizabeth, and Kelly, Gerald R. *Miss Elizabeth: A Memoir.* Boston: Little, Brown & Co., 1969. Memories, not always reliable, of Young's early days in New York.

Arthos, John. "In Honor of Stark Young." *Shenandoah* 5 (Summer 1954):14–27. A perceptive essay stressing the quality of Young's writing and influences upon him.

Bentley, Eric. "An American Theatre Critic! (or the China in the Bull Shop)." *Kenyon Review* 12 (Winter 1950):138–47. A splendid essay on Young's criticism by one of Young's friends.

————. *In Search of Theatre.* New York: Atheneum, 1975. Reprints article in *Kenyon Review.*

————. "Stark Young." *Theatre* (Yale) 14 (Winter 1982):47–53. Lecture delivered at Stark Young Centennial, University of Mississippi, Oxford, Mississippi, 11 October 1981. Valuable assessment of Young's drama criticism and personality.

Bledsoe, Charles Adair. "A Critical Study of Stark Young's Fiction." Master's thesis, Vanderbilt University, 1956. Helpful though limited analysis.

Burns, George Frank. "The Influence of Southern Agrarianism in the Novels of Stark Young." Ph.D. diss., Vanderbilt University, 1973. Extensive discussion of agrarian themes in Stark Young's fiction.

Childrey, Frank Wilson, Jr. "Stark Young: Playwright." Ph.D. diss., University of Mississippi, 1976. The most comprehensive treatment of the subject.

Commager, Henry Steele. "Traditionalism in American Literature." *Nineteenth Century* 146 (November 1949):311–26. Emphasizes the traditional moral elements in Young's writing and compares him to Ellen Glasgow and others.

Davidson, Donald. "Counterattack, 1930–1940; The South against Leviathan." In *Southern Writers in the Modern World,* 31–62. Athens: University of Georgia Press, 1958. An account of the issues and personalities involved in the agrarian controversy.

————. "*I'll Take My Stand:* A History." *American Review* 5 (May 1935):301–21. A firsthand account from perhaps the most active organizer of the agrarian manifesto.

————. *The Spyglass: Views and Reviews, 1924–1930.* Edited by John Tyree Fain. Nashville: Vanderbilt University Press, 1963. Reprints earlier review of *River House.*

_____. *Still Rebels, Still Yankees, and Other Essays.* Baton Rouge: Louisiana State University Press, 1972. Discusses theme and method in *So Red the Rose.*

_____. "The Trend of Literature." In *Culture in the South,* edited by W. T. Couch, 183–210. Chapel Hill: University of North Carolina Press, 1934. Deals with Young's place in Southern literature.

Drexler, Malcolm Burton. "Stark Young's Ideas on Theatre Practice." Ph.D. diss., University of Illinois, 1964. Excellent explication of Young's statements on theatre practice.

Fain, John Tyree, and Young, Thomas Daniel, eds. *The Literary Correspondence of Donald Davidson and Allen Tate.* Athens: University of Georgia Press, 1974. Contains important references to Young.

Harbour, Charles Clayton. "Criteria for Stark Young's Dramatic Criticism." Master's thesis, University of Mississippi, 1959. A sound study written with the advice of Young.

Isaacs, Edith J. R. "The Theatre of Stark Young." *Theatre Arts,* 26 (April 1942):256–65. Young does not write well about bad productions; he is keenly responsive to "everything that has freshness and vitality."

Kyle, John W. "Reconstruction in Panola County." *Mississippi Historical Society* 13 (1913):9–93. Excellent material for Young's background in Como.

Lagner, Lawrence. *The Magic Curtain.* New York: E. P. Dutton & Co., 1951. Deals briefly with Young.

Laster, Ann Appleton. "Stark Young: A Study of His Interest in Italy and the Influence of Italy on His Life and His Works." Master's thesis, University of Mississippi, 1966. Deals effectively with the Italian influence upon Young.

Lumianski, Robert M. "Stark Young and His Dramatic Criticism." Ph.D. diss., Michigan State University, 1955. Account of Young's life and study of his criticism has the advantage of Young's comments on the manuscript.

McAlexander, Hubert Horton, Jr. "Tradition in the Novels of Stark Young." Master's thesis, University of Mississippi, 1966. Sympathetic treatment of the subject.

Mencken, H[enry] L[ouis]. *Prejudices: Second Series.* New York: Alfred A. Knopf, 1920. Mencken's attack upon the South.

Mitchell, Margaret. *Margaret Mitchell's "Gone with the Wind" Letters, 1936–1949.* Edited by Richard Harwell. New York: Macmillan, 1976. Includes Mitchell's letters to Stark Young.

Payne, L. W., Jr. "A New Southern Poet, Stark Young of Mississippi." *South Atlantic Quarterly* 8 (October 1909):316–27. Enthusiastic evaluation of Young's early published and some unpublished poetry.

Rock, Virginia. "The Making and Meaning of *I'll Take My Stand: A Study in Utopian Conservatism.*" Ph.D. diss., University of Minnesota, 1961. Helpful comments on Young's relation to other Agrarians and his contribution.

Rubin, Louis D., Jr. *The Wary Fugitives: Four Poets and the South.* Baton Rouge: Louisiana State University Press, 1978. Analyzes Young's relationship to the Agrarians.

Index